U:P:D:A:T:E

London Docklands
The challenge of develo

Edited by Philip Ogden

Contributors
Andrew Church
Darrel Crilley
John Hall
Ray Hall
Roger Lee
Philip Ogden
Gillian Rose
Matthew Saunders

CAMBRIDGE
UNIVERSITY PRESS

UNIVERSITY OF
LONDON

QUEEN MARY AND WESTFIELD COLLEGE
University of London

Published by the Press Syndicate of the University of Cambridge
The Pitt Building, Trumpington Street, Cambridge CB2 1RP
40 West 20th Street, New York, NY 10011-4211, USA
10 Stamford Road, Oakleigh, Melbourne 3166, Australia

First published 1992
Reprinted 1994

Printed in Great Britain at the University Press, Cambridge

A catalogue record for this book is available from the British Library

ISBN 0 521 42880 7

Update

Update is a unique project in educational publishing. It is aimed at A-level students and first-year undergraduates in geography. The objective of the series, which ranges across both physical and human geography, is to combine the study of major issues in the geography syllabus with accounts of especially significant case studies. Each *Update* incorporates a large amount of empirical material presented in easy-to-read tables, maps and diagrams.

Update is produced from the Department of Geography at Queen Mary and Westfield College (QMW) by an editorial board with expertise from across the fields of Geography and Education. The editor is Roger Lee.

We hope that you find the series as exciting to use as we find it to produce. The editor would be delighted to receive any suggestions for further *Updates* or comments on how we could make the series even more useful and exciting.

Acknowledgements

We are most grateful to the following for permission to reproduce illustrations: London Docklands Development Corporation; Olympia & York Canary Wharf Ltd; Docklands Community Poster Project; the Island History Trust; Tower Hamlets Local History Library.

The editor and authors are most grateful to Edward Oliver for his work on the design of this publication and to Jenn Page for typing several of the chapters.

Preface

No-one who has lived or worked in London during the last decade could be unaware of the dramatic transformation taking place in the London Docklands to the east of the City of London. During the 1980s, some 21 square kilometres bordering the River Thames saw their physical appearance revolutionised: derelict land reclaimed for housing and for commercial development and new transport systems built. The pace and scale of change cannot fail to impress. The latest and the most remarkable symbol of this transformation is the Canary Wharf tower on the Isle of Dogs, topped out in November 1990. Its gradually looming presence, not least over Queen Mary and Westfield College as this book was being planned and brought to fruition, is a confirmation of the impact of change not only on London's East End but also on the economy and geography of London as a whole. It is a powerful reminder of the vast sums of money poured into the area since 1981 – both public and private – and its current financial difficulties underline the fragility of at least some aspects of the redevelopment process.

Certainly, whilst the development of Docklands impresses it also depresses: for some commentators, change has been of benefit to outside interests rather than to those of local residents; the lack of a clear overall plan and the 'spontaneity' of development is a curse rather than a blessing; the architecture is gimmicky and unco-ordinated and the flashiness of the new blocks of housing and offices a facade behind which the original problems of poverty, unemployment and poor housing still lurk.

The Docklands development still has a good way to go before it can be considered complete: the Royal Docks, for example, have scarcely begun to be developed and the Canary Wharf scheme itself will not be completed until well into the 1990s, if ever. Yet the time is ripe for academic interpretations of change in the area to be undertaken: most textbooks on London, or indeed on the regional geography of the UK, need to be revised to take the changes into account.

The *Update* series seems an appropriate vehicle for such an exercise. This volume has been written, therefore, with a Sixth Form or First Year undergraduate audience in mind. The eight contributors cover a variety of topics, though inevitably selectively. As will become evident in reading the volume, there is no general agreement on the balance of pros and cons represented by the redevelopment process: the editor has sought to produce an informative volume and to avoid overlap in the contributions but not to impose a three-line whip on the way in which change is to be interpreted. We hope that the facts and ideas presented here will prove stimulating for those interested in London itself and of value for those concerned with the wider issues of regional changes in the UK and Europe as a whole.

Philip Ogden
London, July 1992

Contents

Road improvements
Who funds the system improvements?
An emerging vision of lower Thamesside
Co-ordination

Acronyms

ALA Association of London Authorities

CRDD Campaign to Restore Democracy in Docklands

DCC Docklands Consultative Committee

DLR Docklands Light Railway

EZ Enterprise Zone

GLC Greater London Council

JDAG Joint Docklands Action Group

LDDC London Docklands Development Corporation

PLA Port of London Authority

STOLport Short Take-Off and Landing airport

UDA Urban Development Area

UDC Urban Development Corporation

Contributors

Andrew Church is Lecturer in Geography at Birkbeck College, University of London. He graduated from the University of Bristol and took his PhD at Queen Mary and Westfield College. He has specialised in the economic geography of the London Docklands and has published a number of papers, dealing especially with changes in employment.

Darrel Crilley was a research student at Queen Mary and Westfield College. He graduated from the University of Oxford in 1988. He has recently completed a PhD thesis on the Docklands and has published articles on the subject in the *Transactions of the Institute of British Geographers* and the *Times Higher Education Supplement*.

John Hall left Queen Mary and Westfield College in 1988 to join the London Boroughs Association, which presents boroughs' views to government on finance, legislation and policy. He became the LBA's first full-time Secretary in 1990. At QMW, his principal research and teaching interests focused on London, especially east London and the Docklands. His publications include a volume in this series, *Metropolis now: London and its region* (CUP, 1990).

Ray Hall is Senior Lecturer in Geography at Queen Mary and Westfield College. She is a population geographer with interests in the UK, including current research on the Docklands, and western Europe. Her publications include two volumes in this series: *World population trends* (1990) and, with Philip Ogden, *Europe's population to the year 2000: the EC and the new Europe* (1993).

Roger Lee is Reader in Geography at Queen Mary and Westfield College. His main interests are in the economic geography of the UK and Western Europe. He has recently contributed to a number of books in these fields, and is the Editor of the *Transactions of the Institute of British Geographers*.

Philip Ogden is Reader in Geography and Head of Department at Queen Mary and Westfield College. His main interests are in the field of population studies, especially migration trends in western Europe. He has recently collaborated with colleagues in QMW and in Paris on a study of migration in inner-city areas, including Docklands.

Gillian Rose teaches social and cultural geography at Queen Mary and Westfield College. Her interest in the East End began with an undergraduate dissertation on the strike at Bryant and May's match factory in Bow in 1888, and continued with postgraduate research into the local politics of Poplar borough in the 1920s.

Matthew Saunders is Secretary of the Ancient Monuments Society and of the Joint Committee of National Amenity Societies. A Cambridge graduate, he has written a number of articles on architectural history, including a biography of the Victorian architect S. S. Teulon.

1 Introduction: some questions of geography and history

Philip Ogden

Reactions and questions

The scale and pace of change in the London Docklands over the last decade is not in doubt. Anyone who visits the area in the early 1990s cannot fail to be impressed by the very visible changes to the landscape and by the sharp contrasts between the glittering new office blocks and housing and the run-down surroundings of much of the Docklands and the adjacent areas. The chapters in this book will, we hope, provide some background for an understanding of the contemporary urban landscape.

As the book was being completed, the London Docklands Development Corporation (LDDC) celebrated its first ten years and the time is therefore ripe for an assessment of the consequences of development policy in the area over that period. Yet it should also be remembered that development even within the LDDC's narrowly defined area is far from complete and that the area immediately around continues to suffer some of the worst symptoms of urban deprivation in the UK.

To assert that the redevelopment of the Docklands under the aegis of the LDDC during the 1980s has proved controversial is an understatement. Consider the following quotations:

> 'It is easy to forget what London Docklands was like ten years ago, and how it might now look without the LDDC. The Corporation was instrumental in opening up East London and the East Thames corridor to investment and recovery . . . LDDC will leave a legacy of new buildings, new infrastructure, new skills and new hope.'
> Michael Heseltine (1991) – then Secretary of State for the Environment (press release on the celebration of the LDDC's tenth anniversary)

> 'The Corporation's expertise and experience in urban regeneration is unparalleled. There is now a real understanding of the needs of the local communities and these will be an integral part of our plans as we move towards the future.'
> LDDC (1988a, p. 5)

> 'We believe that the Docklands' approach offers a useful and positive example to town planning elsewhere. The results speak for themselves. Within ten years Docklands has been transformed from an area of long-term neglect and decay to a vibrant and attractive district which is changing the economic geography of London to the benefit of the whole of East London.'
> David Hardy (1991) – Chair of the LDDC

> 'The so-called regeneration of this area during the 1980s was like a firework display – a spectacular burst of dazzling brilliance followed very quickly by darkness. And the London Docklands Development Corporation is an elegant bejewelled harlot who provides instant attraction and short-term excitement but no long-term satisfaction.'
> Ian Mikardo (1990, p. 11) – for many years a Labour member of parliament.

> 'There was also an instinct that the motive, the regenerative power, was uncaring materialism – to make money not caring about the people who were losing their Docklands. They had lost their jobs way back. Now they were to lose the land and their way of life to incomers and companies who would cream off the profits and then return to their villages in Kent, Sussex and Surrey. Return to a place where they had peace and could leave the world they had created behind them. That is the way many people felt.'
> Jim Thompson (1989, p. 7) – Bishop of Stepney 1978–91

> There is also 'a bitterness, now widely and rightly felt in East London, that far from benefiting from the movement of big capital into the area, locals are being undermined and impoverished by docklands redevelopment.'
> David Widgery (1991, p. 16) – a local GP

> 'The physical emphasis in inner city initiatives the world over performs a screening role . . . a

carnival mask that diverts and entertains,
leaving the social problems that lie behind the
mask unseen and uncared for.'
David Harvey (1989a) – Professor of
Geography at the University of Oxford

These quotations from very different sources –
from a bishop to an academic geographer and from
a prominent government minister to a local GP –
illustrate both the breadth of interest in what has
been happening in the East End of London over the
last decade and also the great range of views
expressed. The significance of Docklands goes
much wider than the area itself. There are five
aspects which make a detailed study of the
redevelopment of the Docklands particularly
rewarding:

(1) It is clear that the experience of Docklands
during the 1980s has wider geographical
significance than simply as another example of
local social and economic change. It is
important for London as a whole and for the
regional geography of the UK. At the time this
book was in its final stages, for example,
Michael Heseltine, the then Secretary of State
for the Environment and the originator of the
Urban Development Corporations (UDCs),
was mooting the idea of massive urban
development along the east Thames corridor,
building on the Docklands expansion and as a
counterbalance to development pressures to the
west of the capital.

(2) The Docklands are also an excellent
illustration of wider developments in society
and economy as they affect the UK, and the
material presented here ties in with discussions
in the discipline of Geography about a number
of issues. For example, the decline in
manufacturing and the rise in service
employment is well illustrated here. In
particular, the rapid increase in the financial
services sector during the 1980s (see, for
example, Harvey, 1989b; Dicken, 1992) has
had a marked effect on the type of jobs being
attracted. The Docklands location next to the
City of London has also had an important
influence on the perception of the area and the
type of activity attracted.

(3) The arrival of new residents may in part be
understood in relation to the wider debate
about 'gentrification', the process by which the
middle classes return to the city centre, and
sometimes displace existing working-class
residents. Certainly one of the most obvious
characteristics of the Docklands is the social
gulf between old and new residents. As
Massey (1991, p. 7) has recently remarked:
'Docklands is in the eye of the storm. In part
that's because of the particular sharpness of the
polarisation – the juxtaposition of terrific
growth and people excluded from it – the two
processes, of apparent improvements on the
one hand, and of exclusion and residualisation
on the other.'

(4) Docklands also illustrates a crucial debate
about the role of planning in inner-city
regeneration and what type of planning there
should be. Should it be 'needs-based', that is
seeking solutions to specific problems of jobs,
housing and so on among the resident
population? Or should development be
'demand-led', that is responsive to the market
and in particular to the private sector? For the
instigators and defenders of the Urban
Development Corporations, set up by the
government in 1981, this second, free-market,
approach was clearly the way forward and
Docklands has become symbolic of the shift in
governmental attitudes and responses
throughout the 1980s. A particularly influential
notion was that of 'leverage' where public
money was used specifically to attract private
capital (see, for example, Brindley, et al.,
1989, pp. 96–120). Detractors of this approach
point not only to the fact that 'demand-led'
planning fails to address social problems but
also that private investment in the area has
required large amounts of public money –
subsidy by any other name – for example in
the form of investments in transport and
service infrastructure and also in the form of
incentives to developers from the public purse,
notably in the Enterprise Zone.

(5) Finally, the particular type of landscape being
created is of interest. This is in relation both to
what happens when detailed planning controls
are relaxed (for example, in the Enterprise
Zone on the Isle of Dogs) and to the general
effects when market forces are unleashed.
Further, the recent interest in trying to define
what characterises the 'Post Modern' city has
highlighted the role of architecture and design,
so that we may find in Docklands some of the
best and the worst of recent buildings. A
particularly interesting theme here is the way
in which architects have made use of both the

physical attributes of the area (the river and docks) and the historical associations (for example, shipping and warehousing) to influence the style and marketing of buildings. So we may seek comparisons with other waterfront redevelopment elsewhere in the world over the last decade as well as with developments in architecture and design in other major world cities (Hoyle, *et al.*, 1988; and see the issue of the *Architectural Review*, vol. 95, no. 1106, 1989, devoted to London and to other cities like Sydney, Hamburg, Barcelona, Copenhagen and Genoa).

Structure of this *Update*

This *Update* is broad in scope, discussing both familiar and innovative issues. It can, nevertheless, cover only in part the questions raised above. After some introductory comments below on the geography and history of the Docklands, Section 1 contains four chapters. The first of these puts Docklands in the context of national and international economic developments. The second looks specifically at the origins and aims of the London Docklands Development Corporation (LDDC) while the third discusses the role of the LDDC in attempting to change the image of the area. Finally, the section closes with an analysis of the rise of opposition to the LDDC and its effectiveness, an aspect too often overlooked. The second section then takes a systematic look at the effects of regeneration on land and property, transport, housing, and employment. The final two chapters look at the demographic changes in the area and at the architectural landscape. We are aware that, in concentrating on *change*, we are led to a certain extent by the priorities and effects of the LDDC and to a narrow geographical focus on the area defined by the Development Corporation. That is why we do not delve into the questions of, for example, education and health, which have remained largely in the hands of the local authorities, though we are not unaware of their significance.

A guide to further reading
The information presented here will, we hope, whet the appetite for reading further. The bibliography at the end of the volume contains, therefore, not only works to which reference is made in the text, but also a wide selection of guides to the area, as well as books and articles, published over the last few years.

The recency of development means that comprehensive academic coverage of the issues is hard to come by. However, there are some promising places to start: Brownill (1990), for example, gives a good overall survey, as do (more briefly) Brindley, *et al.* (1989). Ambrose's (1986) fluent account remains of relevance and the work of Church (1988a and b) provides an authoritative account of the recent impact on employment. The Docklands Consultative Committee (1990) provides a strong critique of the development process. A useful photographic survey, which tells us much about the contrast between the old East End and the new Docklands is presented by Fishman, *et al.* (1990). Telling insights are presented in David Widgery's (1991) portrait of life in the area through the eyes of a local GP and books such as Harvey (1989b) or Hall (1988) provide ambitious attempts to look at economic and social change and the process of planning in very broad geographical and historical contexts.

What are the 'Docklands'?

An important point to grasp at the outset is that despite the temptation to talk about Docklands as a whole – and this is clearly useful for some purposes – we should not forget that the area is very diverse. It consists of a number of well-established and distinctive communities with strong identities based on long histories and, as we shall see below (chapters 3 and 4), the very term 'Docklands' is an invention of recent years. Equally, the nature of development and change in the area since 1981 has been very variable geographically.

Our focus here is not east London as a whole, nor the East End, however that may be defined. Rather, it is the narrowly defined area of the LDDC. At the setting-up of the Development Corporation in 1981, its area was defined as some 21 square kilometres running along the Thames. It impinges on three boroughs: Tower Hamlets and Newham to the north of the river and Southwark to the south. The area included large areas of docks and 90 kilometres of water's edge. There were fewer than 40,000 residents. At the heart of the Isle of Dogs was the Enterprise Zone, where special conditions for developers applied (chapter 3).

The LDDC itself has adopted a four-part division of the area (fig. 1.1):

(1) Wapping, located closest to the City of London and where some redevelopment (at St Katharine's Dock, for example) had begun in the 1970s. A great deal of the development here has been residential (Crilley *et al.*, 1991), including both new building and conversions of riverside warehouses.

(2) The Isle of Dogs, the area of greatest development of non-residential use. Here lies the Enterprise Zone (chapter 3), with the Canary Wharf office complex as the centrepiece. There has also been new residential development on the riverside.

(3) The Royal Docks, located well to the east. A good deal of new housing was built early in the 1980s, for example at Beckton, and the airport lies on a narrow strip of land between the Royal Albert Dock and the King George V Dock to the south. Here is found the greatest remaining potential for development.

(4) The Surrey Docks, located to the south of the Thames and encompassing parts of the old communities of Bermondsey and Rotherhithe. This area was also defined to include a narrow strip of land running along the river westwards as far as London Bridge, so that intensive development for office use (London Bridge City especially) contrasts with up-market warehouse conversions and new housing further east.

Historical background

The controversy surrounding redevelopment arises in part because a new landscape has not been imposed on a blank sheet. Wapping, Shadwell, Limehouse, the Isle of Dogs, Bermondsey, and Rotherhithe have a rich history over centuries rather than decades, arising from their association with the river, with docks, shipping and the allied industries. The areas to the east of Tower Bridge have been the traditional heartland of working-class London. The development of the port, especially from the early nineteenth century, was the key both to the area's character and to the problems which began to gather pace by the third quarter of the twentieth century. Docks opened in quick succession throughout the century (table 1.1), confirming London's role at the heart of commerce within and beyond the Empire. New activities did not come without dislocation to the

local population: the building of St Katharine's in the 1820s, for example, displaced thousands of inhabitants. Above all, though, the expansion of the local economy was accompanied by massive urbanisation. Port activities brought employment both directly and through associated manufacturing and heavy industries, including shipbuilding, engineering and many obnoxious industries not tolerated elsewhere in London (Brindley, *et al.*, 1989, p. 98).

The 'image' of east London – an aspect specifically targeted by the LDDC (chapter 4) – certainly owes its origins to the nineteenth century. Little of the wealth generated made its way to the local population. Employment in the docks was notoriously fragile and the wider area of the East End became synonymous with Victorian poverty, overcrowding and slum housing as revealed in the compelling portrait by Fishman (1988) of the East End a century before. This was the London of Charles Booth's survey of poverty in the 1880s which revealed that in Tower Hamlets 35 per cent of the population 'had been found living, at all times, more or less in want' (Fishman, 1988, p. 3); a London unknown to most residents further west but brought to their attention by writers as diverse as Charles Dickens and Jack London. Fishman (1988, p. 1) quotes J. H. Mackay in *The Anarchists* to great effect. He wrote in 1891: 'The East End of London is the hell of poverty. Like an enormous black, motionless, giant Kraken,[1] the poverty of London lies there in lurking silence and encircles with its mighty tentacles the life and wealth of the City and of the West End'.

Table 1.1   Dates of opening and closure of the major docks

Dock	Date of opening	Date of closure
West India	1802	1980
London	1805	1968
East India	1806	1967
Limehouse Basin	1812	1969
St Katharine's	1828	1969
Royal Victoria	1855	1981
Surrey	1858	1970
Millwall	1868	1980
Royal Albert	1880	1981
King George V	1921	1981

[1] Kraken: a fabled sea monster

5

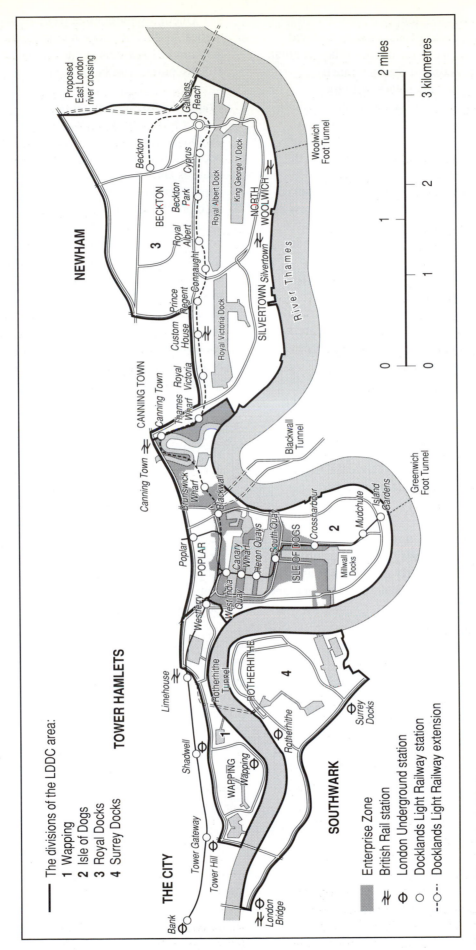

Figure 1.1 Map of the LDDC area.

Despite these traditional images of poverty, the docks did form the basis of an active and varied local economy. The story for much of the twentieth century, however, is one of decline, much accentuated since the later 1960s with the successive closure of dock basins (table 1.1). The reasons for the decline are complex, relating to changes both at the global scale in the nature of international trade and cargo handling and at the local scale in the ownership, control and organisation of the docks. Trade gradually moved eastwards downstream, as more modern, accessible and well-equipped docks opened. London had to compete increasingly not only with Tilbury but with other UK and European ports. Passenger traffic declined rapidly. The growing importance of large ships (for example, for the oil traffic) and of containerisation meant that trade moved rapidly away from the older docks to deep-water terminals, where technology, transport and storage space were available more readily.

By the later 1970s, the Docklands had suffered a period of serious and debilitating economic crisis for which the traditional activities held out no hope of providing a solution. The most important characteristics of the area by the time the LDDC was given the job of regeneration may be summarised as follows:

- a crisis in investment in both the private and public sectors, in industry and in the public services. One particularly marked indication of this was the amount of vacant and derelict land (chapter 6).

- a rapid decline in employment: dock employment in London fell from 25,000 in 1961 to 4100 by 1981 (Church, 1988a, p. 188; and see chapter 9). Further, for every one job lost in the docks, three more were lost in related industries of manufacturing, ship repair and transport. There was a 27 per cent decline in employment in the Docklands area between 1978 and 1981 alone (Brindley, *et al.*, 1989, p.

98). Unemployment rates were amongst the highest in the UK: male unemployment stood at around 21 per cent in the Docklands area by 1981 (Church, 1988a, p. 188).

- a rapid decline in population: by around a quarter between 1971 and 1981. Many parts of the Docklands boroughs had been losing population since the 1930s to overspill estates, suburbs and New Towns. However, the rate of population loss accelerated. There was also a high proportion of single-person households in some areas and considerable ageing of the population as out-migration accompanied job losses. Even by the standards of inner London as a whole, which was experiencing sharp out-migration during this period, Docklands was exceptional.

- social deprivation in housing, education and health: for example, Ambrose (1986, p. 246) quotes an estimate that in the early 1970s 15 per cent of families in the area claimed welfare benefits, compared to the Greater London average of 5 per cent. In addition, there was a very high proportion of the population in public housing – 83 per cent of households in 1981 (LDDC, 1991b, p. 46) and much of that housing was of a poor standard, especially the estates of flats and tower blocks built during the 1950s and 1960s in response to the extensive war damage and the slum clearance programmes. There was also a growing problem of homelessness within the three Dockland boroughs.

These problems had, of course, been recognised well before the advent of the LDDC in 1981 and, as chapter 3 shows, schemes for redevelopment were devised from the later 1960s onwards. However, the LDDC marked a radical departure in the way in which development was to be approached, as we shall see below. The quotations at the start of this chapter give some indication of the controversies surrounding this approach and its results.

2 London Docklands: the 'exceptional place'?
An economic geography of inter-urban competition

Roger Lee

Introduction: the Docklands: an 'exceptional place'?

Whatever else it may entail, the redevelopment of London's Docklands has involved a dramatic transformation of an urban landscape. The intensity and scale of this newly created urban imagery (chapters 4 and 6) has already served to place the area on the itinerary of almost one in five of London's overseas visitors. Docklands has become a kind of urban Disneyworld – a world which invites a temporary suspension of disbelief. And such a reaction is far from unintended. The quotation in the title of this chapter is taken from one of the publicity leaflets published by the LDDC. The Corporation is fond of creating images of Docklands as a unique area but draws only selectively from the rich industrial and social history of the place (chapter 5).

The notion of an 'exceptional place' carries with it the idea that Docklands is really quite different from other places. It is meant to suggest that the dramatic developments that have taken place there are the consequence of the self-regenerative powers released (by the genie of the LDDC) within Docklands during the 1980s. It has been a short step from such a view to the representation of Docklands nationally and internationally as a symbol of liberal economic policies and of enterprise liberated by the operation of market forces, constrained only by judicious interventions from an Urban Development Corporation (UDC) committed to facilitating and subsidising private investment.

Some unexceptional realities of Docklands development

Throughout the first half of 1992 disbelief was forcibly suspended as the prosaic financial realities behind the spectacular visual entertainment offered by Docklands became ever more insistent. Paradoxically, it is the most spectacular manifestation of redevelopment in Docklands – the 29 hectares of Canary Wharf – which presented the most dramatic testimony to these realities.

Located in the former West India Docks, Canary Wharf took its name from one of its former specialisms, the import of fruit from the Canary Islands. Today it is the scene of an audacious but flawed attempt to build a business centre in Docklands to rival the City of London and the West End. In the sixteen days between 2 July and 17 July 1987 Olympia & York (O & Y, a private Canadian company and one of the largest property developers in the world) secured Canary Wharf from G. Ware Travelstead and their investment bankers, who were pulling out of a redevelopment proposal, and signed an agreement with the LDDC to develop the site. A phased development programme to construct 10.9 million square feet of commercial, retail, office and hotel space was begun. The scheme is so big that it has come to dominate, even determine, the future prospects not only of Docklands but of the wider but diffuse and ill-coordinated attempt to shift the geography of growth in London away from the west towards the east Thames corridor.

By June 1992 four million square feet – including Cesar Pelli's tower, which is the second largest skyscraper in Europe – were complete, but only 57 per cent of the space was let (at extremely low rentals), with 14 per cent of the space actually occupied. At the end of the previous March, O & Y had been forced by the downgrading of their credit rating in Canada to admit a liquidity crisis and to announce that negotiations had begun to restructure the repayment of their world-wide debts which by June 1992 stood at a level of $11.2 billion.

Canary Wharf.   Photo: LDDC

Given the global complexity of O &Y's operations, it was anticipated that the restructuring would take about two years to complete. But just over seven weeks later, on 14 May, O & Y were forced to file for insolvency protection in North America in order to secure their assets from their creditors. Less than a fortnight later, the Canary Wharf project (formally the responsibility of Olympia & York Canary Wharf Ltd.), which had cost £1.4 billion to June 1992, including bank borrowings of just over £1.1 billion, was placed in administration. Given the depressed state of the office market in London in which tenants will remain difficult to find for a decade at least, realistic rentals might amount to £15 per square foot, and there is clearly a need to take a long-term view (a period of around 15 years) of what is a risky investment. One estimate of the current (June 1992) value of Canary Wharf is between £150 and £200 million (Houlder, 1992b) and two potential buyers had indicated that the value of the projects was no more than £600 million (*The Financial Times*, 7 June 1992). How can we begin to explain this spectacular collapse?

Clearly, Canary Wharf is the product of the operation of a powerful range of forces underpinning the creation of the urban built environment whose provenance lies far beyond Docklands and its policies of urban regeneration. Despite the financial inducements to development offered by the Isle of Dogs Enterprise Zone (chapter 3) and the bending of public infrastructure programmes in London to serve Canary Wharf (see below and chapter 7), its origins do not lie in local or national policies of urban renewal. Indeed, it would be futile to try to understand Canary Wharf simply from the perspective and operation of policies for the redevelopment of the inner city.

The sheer scale, significance, symbolism and hoped-for stature of Canary Wharf as a global business location all point to and derive from developments in the global economy. It is the working of global financial and property markets, and the power of a developer like Olympia & York to see the potential for profitability in property development represented by the dynamics of these markets, that underpin the scheme. One of the purposes of this chapter is to outline the ways in which such a process of urban redevelopment takes place.

The redevelopment of Docklands beyond Canary Wharf – a process influenced more directly by the

LDDC and urban policy – is also as prosaic as it is spectacular. Certainly it is uneven in both space and time. 'The "miracle" of Docklands', according to Brian Robson (1988, p. 125), 'is miraculous only because it has taken so long to materialize'. The formal closure of the docks began in the late 1960s and ministerial concern for the area had been voiced as early as 1971 (chapter 3). Similarly, if the House of Lords Select Committee on the LDDC (1981, p. 11) believed that the creation of a UDC was necessary to ensure 'a single minded concern for the regeneration of the 'docklands' as a whole', questions arise about the subsequent uneven geography of development. Nearly 70 per cent of office space in Docklands is located within the Enterprise Zone and, far from redeveloping the Docklands area as a whole, the LDDC has demonstrated a clear-headed understanding of the economic geography of profitability within Docklands and has planned developments accordingly:

> 'the Corporation looks to see that each site in Docklands is used to its maximum economic potential. This may imply that some forms of new development, such as low-cost housing and light industrial development would tend not to be located on the river front, but rather on inland sites.' (LDDC, 1987, p. 7)

Clearly, the subtle geography of the attractiveness of Docklands to capital is well appreciated by the 'planning' authority and this geography has influenced redevelopment in Docklands, which has, in consequence, been extremely patchy (chapters 1 and 6).

This chapter seeks to offer a more dispassionate way of seeing than that encouraged by Docklands hyperbole. This more realistic view comes from understanding the underlying realities of the economic geography of Docklands. It is necessarily concerned with the question of what the redevelopment of Docklands is for. It concludes that the answer to this question has little to do with an attempt to redistribute wealth to the inhabitants of a deprived inner-city district and everything to do with the sustenance and expansion of Britain's and London's role in the global economy. However, the chapter also concludes that success in the achievement of this goal is highly questionable.

Docklands, London, and the economic geography of inter-urban competition

Although not exceptional, the Docklands of London are not just any inner-city area. The Isle of Dogs is less than five kilometres from the City of London and the western border of the UDC at St Katharine's Dock adjoins the City. It should come as no surprise then that the redevelopment of St Katharine's was already well towards completion by 1981 when the UDC was created, or that this redevelopment is dominated by commercial activities. The bases of redevelopment in Docklands lie in the significance of London as a global centre of finance and business services and in the profitable potential of property development to extend London's competitive position as a world city.

By 1955 Britain was 'one of the most highly industrialised economies the capitalist world has ever seen' (Rowthorn, 1986, p. 3). Since that time, and in line with well-established general trends in changing employment patterns as economic development proceeds, the percentage of those in industrial employment has fallen whilst employment in services has expanded. Between 1959 and 1981 employment in services in Britain grew by nearly 23 per cent compared to a fall of over 26 per cent in production industries and over 13 per cent in transport and communications. By contrast, employment in insurance, banking and financial services grew over the same period by over 107 per cent (Rowthorn and Wells, 1987). Employment growth in London as a whole between 1981 and 1987 has been increasingly concentrated upon a narrow range of producer services – most especially banking, finance and business services (Frost, 1991) – a dependency which has a number of effects. For example, at the global level, it exposes the economy of London to the vicissitudes of change in such activities and intensifies the competition between London and other cities as locations for them.

Such inter-urban competition (Harvey, 1985) is part cause and part consequence of increased integration within the world economy during the 1980s. This was a period during which, after the recession of 1980–81, the growth in world trade in manufactures and services consistently outstripped the growth in production thereby increasing global financial transactions, and in which financial deregulation led to a marked increase in the flows of capital around the world economy. At the same time, the activities of multinational corporations sustained their global significance and increasingly international origins but were supported by a growing range of specialist service providers whose activities and growth were aided by rapid developments in information technology and telecommunications.

The geographical requirements of such developments are for cities offering the range of instant knowledge and efficient markets necessary to ensure close integration into the world economy and to conduct business in an efficient manner. Of secondary importance is adequate provision of trading and office spaces necessary to enable the heightened level and pace of transactions to take place. But the stakes are high. Thus the Bank for International Settlements (BIS, 1991) has argued that the rapid increase in global flows of capital during the 1980s was a one-off phenomenon closely related to deregulation within the major

financial centres induced by inter-urban competition. But the effect of such increases was far from insignificant. They induced over-optimistic forecasts of continued growth and of demand for office space in London and other major financial centres as well as releasing surplus capital which could be channelled into property development.

Such trends have been especially significant for Docklands. The area is located next to one of the three great world cities of contemporary capitalism (London, New York, Tokyo) and yet in an inner-city locality formerly dominated by employment in industry and transport (chapter 9) and which is one of the most deprived areas of London. Within the London labour market, the increased specialisation on a narrow range of producer services shifts the demand for skills away from those characteristic of the locality, reduces the possibilities of part-time working and polarises growth in the central area of London (Frost, 1991).

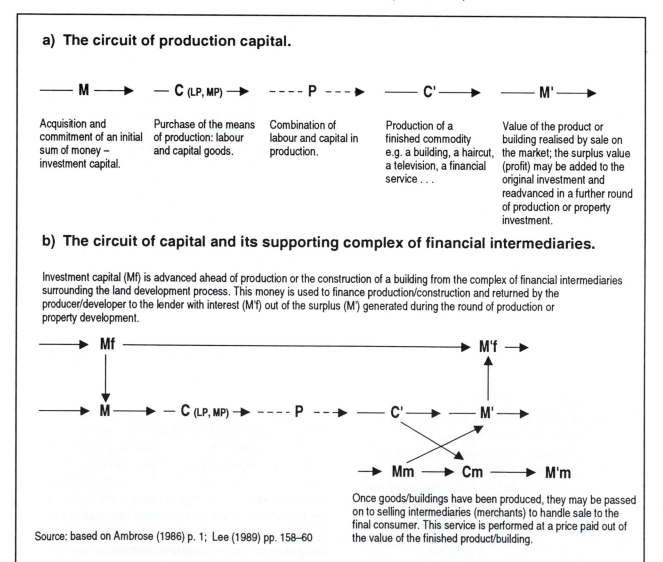

Figure 2.1   The circuit of capital and the production of the built environment.

Against such a background, the rest of this chapter sets out an interpretation of how it is that urban transformation and redevelopment – such as that exemplified by Docklands – takes place. It tries to answer the question of how geography (in this case, the geography of Docklands) is made. In fact, there are two questions here. What are the general conditions for the construction of the built environment? And what influences its construction and redevelopment in particular locations – in our case, Docklands? The further question of how we might evaluate such developments is addressed in the concluding sections of the chapter.

Making urban landscapes

The land development process

Land development involves the commitment of an initial sum of money (investment capital); the acquisition and preparation of land (including the provision of adequate means of access to and from the land – chapter 6); the construction of the new built environment; and its sale or rent to an end user or institutional owner investing in property as part of an investment portfolio. The process of construction and development may be undertaken by end users of the property – either directly, or indirectly with the use of sub-contractors – for their own occupation. More generally, the development of land for profit takes place in a speculative fashion with property development companies acquiring land, organising construction companies to undertake the building, and then marketing the product by placing the newly complete or semi-complete built environment on to the property market in the expectation that it will be bought by others for their own use or as a means of further speculation. This sequence describes a single round of production of the built environment and the profit resulting from it may then be used for consumption, for investment in a further round of production or for investment in other forms of economic activity. Successive rounds of production enable the accumulation of capital by the successful investors. Looked at in this way, 'the development of land for profit is simply a special case of the process by which entrepreneurs seek to accumulate wealth' (Ambrose, 1986, p.1)

The major processes involved in the making of the built environment conform to the circuit of capital (Lee, 1989). Figure 2.1 offers a schematic representation of one round of production within the circuit of capital. It is drawn deliberately to emphasise the point that the development of land for profit is a special case of the process of production in general within capitalist societies. The crucial point to note from figure 2.1 is that the purpose of investment in capitalist societies is the accumulation of further capital, and the measure of the worth and value of such investment is the rate of profit that it is able to achieve within each round of production. The allocation of investment capital to the production of the built environment has, therefore, to compete with other uses of capital which may be more profitable – at least in the short run.

There is, then, nothing automatic or inevitable about this process; rather it has involved a complex set of relations within the wider capitalist economy and between the economy and the British state.

The land development process and the wider economy

The making of the built environment involves a great deal of money. By July 1991, the redevelopment of Docklands had involved the switching of £8.4 billion of private capital into the creation of its new built environment (Cassell, 1991). It is in the nature of property development that much of the money is required 'up-front' with a relatively long lead-time elapsing during the land acquisition and construction phases before the investment begins to pay off.

Where does the capital for investment in the (re)development of the built environment come from? During the early 1920s, Edsel Ford, then President of the Ford Motor Company in Detroit, decided to build an office block to house an expanded sales team and the company's accounting staff. His father, Henry Ford I, not only stopped the construction of the new building – which had already begun – but evicted the accounts department from their existing cramped quarters. This was in part a power struggle between father and son (Lacey, 1986, p. 264) but it also reflects an underlying economic tension: money used to develop the built environment cannot be used to further direct production. As the inventor of mass production in the automobile industry, Henry Ford was unable to recognise the need to commit resources to strategy and close administration in an expanding business. His perception was that such a project simply served to absorb scarce capital in a non-productive activity when it could be used to build more cars.

However, unless this distinction between what David Harvey (1978) calls the primary circuit of capital (that directly involved in the production of commodities and the maintenance of a labour force) and a secondary circuit involving the production of capital goods and the means of consumption (such as consumer durables) on the one hand, and the creation of the built environment for production and consumption on the other, is kept in reasonable balance, the smooth operation of the economy as a whole may be threatened. In the case of Ford, Henry's aversion to investment in anything other than the primary circuit (direct production of the Model T) created serious problems for the company and allowed its rivals to catch up and overtake what had seemed only a few years earlier an unassailable position.

Capital might be switched towards the construction of the built environment if the profitability of the latter is high relative to other investment possibilities. But in any case the inherent need for large amounts of capital in the process of land development necessitates the existence of 'a functioning capital market and, perhaps, a state willing to finance and guarantee long-term, large-scale projects with respect to the creation of the built environment' (Harvey, 1978, p.107). Even if relative levels of profitability make investment in the built environment attractive to capital, there is a need for a set of mechanisms to create liquid capital capable of being switched into the secondary circuit in suitable quantities at the right time and in the right place. Financing of this sort requires a money supply and credit system which can create 'fictional capital' (Harvey, 1978, p 107), made available in advance of the production of the built environment. And there may be a need for some forms of state support of such investment – especially if it is taking place in locations or at times which are less than auspicious.

A complex of financial intermediaries has grown up around the land development industry to manage its finances. One of the most basic of the jobs facing property finance is to provide the capital to enable the land development process to proceed. This is no easy task because the land development business is notoriously susceptible to cyclical fluctuations (fig. 2.2). The growth of office rentals provides one indicator of this characteristic fluctuation. In 1989 office rentals in the UK grew by almost 30 per cent having risen from a rate of less than 5 per cent in 1985 but scarcely exceeded a 10 per cent growth rate in 1990.

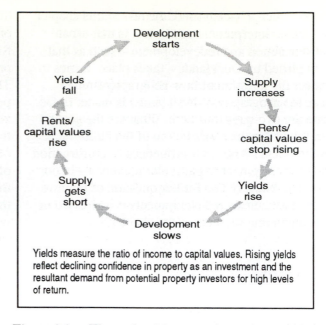

Yields measure the ratio of income to capital values. Rising yields reflect declining confidence in property as an investment and the resultant demand from potential property investors for high levels of return.

Figure 2.2   The cycle of property investment.

The financial system is itself a major factor in exacerbating, if not causing, the cyclical behaviour of the property market. According to Houlder (1990) the property boom of the late 1980s was a product of a combination of factors including the growing obsolescence of London offices in an age of electronic information technology, an apparent increase in the demand for open-plan offices triggered by global financial markets, a marked increase in the availability of large new tracts of land (such as at Broadgate in the City but most especially in Docklands) and, most importantly, the availability of new sources of credit and techniques of property financing. Over 40 per cent of the fictional capital advanced to property development during 1990 emanated from foreign – most notably Japanese – banks (fig. 2.3).

The tumultuous nature of property boom and slump in the UK is due in part to the global role of London as a financial centre attracting credit available for property development from around the world. But, at the same time, the flow of international investment in completed property is much slower, smaller, more lumpy and more volatile than the flow of loan capital. As a result, property development was over-stimulated during the later 1980s but the excess supply was not absorbed by institutional investors (despite large inflows of investment from Sweden and Japan) so contributing to high vacancies, depressed rentals and high yields. Yields are currently at an all-time high in London – although prime sites still compare favourably with cities elsewhere in Europe. But yields in London rose throughout the

1980s as the proportion of institutional investment portfolios devoted to property fell from 18 to 11 per cent (Houlder, 1990).

Figure 2.3 charts a number of indicators of the relative attractiveness of the property sector for investment capital during the 1980s. It shows that the redevelopment of Docklands took place against the background of a property boom in the UK. The boom peaked in 1988 as a consequence in part of a growing imbalance of supply and demand for office space, but continued to attract large amounts of loan capital from banks until 1990 with property loans approaching 10 per cent of all loans by mid 1990 after which there was a spectacular withdrawal of capital from the property market.

In April 1992, the vacancy rate for offices in central London (including Docklands) was 18 per cent of available space, with over 34 million square feet empty – the equivalent of 190 office blocks the size of London's Centre Point (Houlder,

1992a). In Docklands, the vacancy rate is around 50 per cent and in Canary Wharf over 40 per cent. The fall in demand for space induced in part by the recession which began in 1989–90 came at the same time as an increase in space was arriving in the market. The rising levels of interest rates during the later 1980s and in 1990 inhibited institutional investment in property and caused both rents and capital values of property portfolios to fall, whilst yields rose to historically high levels and the value of property shares fell.

An immediate consequence was that many property development companies with access to far smaller reserves and credit than O & Y were suddenly exposed. During 1990, for example, over 650 property companies in the United Kingdom went into liquidation and the fate of the biggest property company in the world remained tied to the possibilities of attracting fresh capital into Canary Wharf and of securing tenants to fill its empty spaces.

The land development process, the wider economy and the state
It is no accident that the pace and scale of development in Docklands matches the trajectory of boom and slump in the property market. So it should come as no surprise to read headlines like *Developer of Canary Wharf in plea to PM* over a story which details an appeal direct to Mr John Major 'for government help to ensure the success of the recession-hit office complex in London's Docklands' (Stephens, 1991). The involvement of the state in the creation of the built environment has been alluded to briefly already. In the case of the redevelopment of the London Docklands, the state has been particularly important. The use of a term such as 'demand-led' planning (chapter 3) should not obscure the role of the state in attracting, subsidising and underpinning capital investment.

As an Urban Development Corporation, the LDDC is free from the social obligations and expenses of local authorities and, in being financed directly from central government and so sidestepping the chronic fiscal shortfalls of inner-city local authorities, is able to pursue the unambiguous objectives of economic redevelopment and encouragement to the private sector. Large amounts of public money from the central state are involved in this process of persuading sources of capital that Docklands is a suitable place for investment.

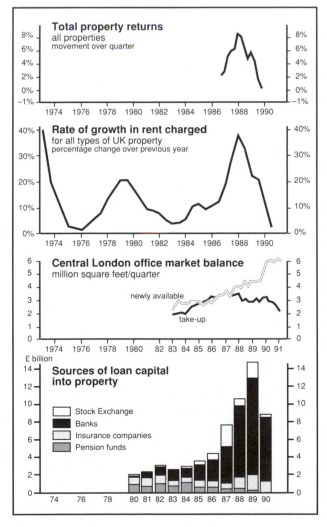

Figure 2.3   The dynamics of the property market.

Table 2.1 London Dockland's share of urban development funds in the UK, 1981/2 to 1990/1 (£m)

Year	LDDC	All UDCs	Urban total	LDDC share of total %
1981/82	31	38	162	19
1982/83	41	62	283	14
1983/84	62	94	325	19
1984/85	58	88	450	13
1985/86	57	86	436	13
1986/87	65	89	429	15
1987/88	83	134	483	17
1988/89	116	234	559	25
1989/90	256	436	760	34
1990/91	333	550	905	37

Sources: *Financial Times*, 21 February 1991; *Hansard*, 14 February 1991.

This persuasion takes two forms:

(1) making the area ready to receive capital by creating an environment attractive to private investors through the provision of the necessary but very expensive and unprofitable infrastructure without which little if any capital could be attracted; and

(2) offering large subsidies to private capital in the Isle of Dogs Enterprise Zone in the form of rate-free premises, capital tax allowances and freedom from planning restrictions.

The LDDC has absorbed a large and rapidly growing proportion of the money spent by the state on urban development (table 2.1). Despite this rapid increase in its income, the LDDC was in financial deficit in 1989/90. Like the other UDCs, the LDDC has been instructed by the Department of the Environment to prepare to wind up its operations by 1993/94 or 1997/98.

The LDDC has spent much of its money on improving the image of Docklands, on land preparation and acquisition and on infrastructural improvements (chapters 3, 4 and 6). Furthermore, the political need for success in the redevelopment of Docklands has such a hold on national government thinking that it shapes its decision making. The then Minister of State for Transport, Mr Roger Freeman, made a week-long visit to Docklands in September 1991. The visit was prompted by criticisms from Docklands developers – especially Olympia & York – about the inadequacy of the area's transport links. His response at the end of his visit to such criticism of, for example, the Docklands Light Railway (DLR,

chapter 7) was that 'taxpayers' money is not a constraint to the solution of this problem', whereas when, seconds later, he was asked about the identified needs for massive expenditure throughout the London Underground system he responded 'there must be a limit to the taxpayer'. Richard Tomkins (1991) concludes that the 'juxtaposition of those two statements comes as a sharp reminder of the fact that investment in the capital's creaking and overburdened transport infrastructure is dwarfed by the money going on transport in Docklands', on the upgrading and extensions to the DLR, on the proposed extension of the Jubilee Line and on a number of expensive road schemes.

One of the ways in which the LDDC measures its own success is by calculating a 'leverage ratio' which purports to show how much private capital has been attracted to Docklands for each pound of publicly financed expenditure by the Corporation. At first sight, this indicator of success looks impressive and some now claim a ratio of about 12:1. But, as the DCC (1990) points out, there are two sets of major qualifications which must be made to this assessment. First, the accuracy of the LDDC's measurements of leverage ratios is open to question as they include and exclude items in an arbitrary, not to say biased, fashion. Not included in the calculation are the rate allowances or the capital tax allowances applicable in the Isle of Dogs Enterprise Zone which has attracted the largest amount of capital in the UDC. Nor do the calculations include spending by the Department of Transport on road improvements and public transport in Docklands. And yet transportation is, as we have seen, critical to the long-term success of property redevelopment in Docklands.

Similarly, the expenditure made in Docklands by the local authorities and the DJC before the advent of the LDDC is excluded notwithstanding the fact that the House of Lords Select Committee on the LDDC (1981, p. 13) were 'impressed by the amount which has in fact been achieved by the DJC and the boroughs despite the unfavourable economic climate'.

But what is included in the calculation is the effect of the increase in land values in Docklands which has certainly benefited the LDDC, but only to the extent that it has been able to realise the increase in land values when selling on land to private developers. Once sold, of course, any further appreciation in value accrues to the new owners – no matter what the source of that increase in value. Increases in land values are, of course, closely related to the process of development in Docklands itself, but that in turn was driven by the property boom throughout south-east England during the mid to late 1980s. With the collapse of the property boom in 1989–90, leverage values have fallen, so indicating not only the misleading nature of their calculation but also that developments in Docklands are closely tied to developments elsewhere in the economy rather than being accounted for by an 'exceptional' Docklands factor.

The second qualification to the interpretation of the leverage ratios is simply that, as the National Audit Office and the DCC have argued, the unusually high ratios raise the question of whether it was necessary to spend so much to attract private capital into Docklands. The implication here is that any leverage has been of public money by private capital rather than the other way round. The financing of the DLR and its extension and the extension of the Jubilee Line into Docklands merely serve to confirm this view, with private-sector contributions to the latter amounting to nothing like the 40 per cent originally claimed by the Department of Transport.

Docklands and inter-urban competition in the global economy

It is one thing to build a new urban environment and quite another to transform a built environment created during previous rounds of production and now abandoned by the circuit of capital. What has been the rationale for the successive decisions by central government to continue to underwrite and promote the redevelopment of Docklands?

One set of reasons concerns the political and ideological commitment to an inner-city policy driven by the demands of investment capital; another the attempt to try to reverse the unbalanced growth to the west and east of London; a third relates to the commitment of a capitalist state to the interests of capital and the need to sustain policies which facilitate profitability and successful accumulation. This is one of the reasons why Olympia & York, in particular, has been so successful in gaining effective access to the state. A fourth reason for continued state involvement in the fortunes of Docklands lies in the concern of the state for the competitive position of London as a global financial centre – a centre which acts as a location for some of the most powerful components of the circuit of capital, those involved in the global allocation and switching of capital around the world economy. It is this latter point that will provide the focus of the rest of this chapter.

Cities and financial markets
Cities are not mere passive receptacles of economic activity, they are the means through which economic activity in the form of the circuit of capital takes place. Cities have always been crucial to the functioning and geographical organisation of the world economy. London, for example, is shifting economically – if not politically – from its role as imperial city and major concentration of industry to that of a global metropolis through which the financial exchanges of the world economy take place (King, 1990).

The effect of this restructuring of capital did not escape east London. Indeed, the disinvestment associated with the successive closure of the docks and the rationalisation of inner-city industry in the face of the economic crisis of the 1970s had a profoundly depressive effect on the economic performance of London. This was especially marked in inner East London, coming as it did on top of 50 years of decline in the basic industries of the district and the failure to replace these industries with sufficient new development to help offset decline (Howick and Key, 1978).

In the contemporary world, major cities such as London are the places in which the complex of financial institutions and economic control centres such as the headquarters of major national and international corporations may cluster, and their decisions shape the flow of capital through the global economy (Lee, 1989). In an increasingly integrated global economy (Thrift, 1989), the significance of world cities such as London tends to increase not only because the circuit of capital is itself increasingly world-wide and demands 24-hour trading in financial markets (so requiring three global centres – currently London, New York and Tokyo) but also because such a global economy necessitates a highly specialised and sensitive set of control mechanisms. These may be provided only in cities of the highest rank. Such global control centres assume more and more significance as the complexity of the world-wide circuit of capital both requires sophisticated management and decision-making and enables a multitude of profitable transactions at what are in effect the nerve centres of the world economy.

One of London's major advantages in this regard is its ability to operate on a multicurrency basis. More money changes hands each day in foreign currency transactions than in any other market and London remains the largest global centre for foreign exchange dealing. According to figures

Photo: Olympia & York

The view from the newly-landscaped public spaces of Canary Wharf over the Thames towards the City of London.

from the Bank for International Settlements (McCallum 1991), the total daily turnover in global currency markets during 1989 was $640 billion, of which the UK (in effect, London) took almost 30 per cent, the US (New York) 20 per cent and Japan (Tokyo) 18 per cent. The foreign exchange market in London is 45 per cent larger than New York and 63 per cent greater than Tokyo. The scale of such trading sets London apart from any European competitor and will help to sustain its role as a global city into the foreseeable future. By way of contrast, London's global role as a centre of equity (stocks and shares) management is nowhere near as dominant as New York and, especially, Tokyo. This is due in part to the competition to London emanating from smaller stock markets elsewhere in Europe – Geneva, Zurich, Paris and Frankfurt.

The banking, finance, insurance and business services sector, employing almost three-quarters of a million people, is the largest employer in Greater London, accounting for one-fifth of total employment. Until recently, it was also the fastest growing sector: four-fifths of the growth of a quarter of a million employees in the sector since 1971 occurred since 1978. The expansion of this sector has been closely influenced by London's international role, as foreign banks accounted for half the growth in employment in finance (excluding insurance) in the City of London between the late 1970s and the mid 1980s (London Chamber of Commerce, 1989).

Nevertheless, the spectacular growth in employment in business services during the late 1980s has come to a shuddering stop. Recent estimates (Local Economic Policy Unit, 1991) suggest that employment in business services, banking and insurance fell by nearly 150,000 during the year from March 1990 and that employment in these sectors will show a net decline of about 40,000 jobs over the next nine years. These figures imply that the response by business and financial services firms to the significance of the factors (including the growth of specialist business services, the deregulation of the financial markets ('big bang') and the growth of information technologies enabling customised service provision) underlying the boom in business and financial services jobs during the 1980s was an over-reaction. However, the decline in employment does not necessarily mean that London's competitiveness as a location for such activity is in decline.

Docklands and the competitive ability of London
From the outset, the redevelopment of Docklands has been seen as a means of increasing the competitive advantage of London internationally. According to the then Secretary of State for the Environment when instituting the LDDC in 1981, Docklands 'represents a major opportunity for the development that London needs over the last twenty years of the twentieth century' (quoted in LDDC, 1988). Thus, the promotion of Docklands is justified not by the needs of the local people who have been isolated economically and geographically by the closure of the docks but by the needs of the national economy centred on the global functions of London and by the requirements of private capital.

The concern for national rather than local problems, for the problems of private capital rather than local residents, and with the reaffirmation of the view that the role of the state is to provide the means for profitable investment, is made quite clear in the Report of the House of Lords Select Committee on the LDDC (1981, p. 11). This report endorses the government's view that the decline of Docklands 'created a problem which may fairly be called a national rather than a local one', and points out that capital flows only into places and projects which make an adequate profit: 'private investors will not put money into docklands on any large scale unless they are encouraged by an environment attractive to them'.

This argument is then used to legitimise the expenditure of large amounts of public money. It is an argument taken up by Michael Heseltine, who, when designating the UDC and justifying the heavy financial involvement of the central state in what is supposed to be a capital-led process of regeneration, asserted that Docklands represents a national economic problem rather than a local problem of social regeneration: 'this transformation from decline to renewal . . . can only be achieved by a level of public expenditure that only the Exchequer can afford' (LDDC, 1987, p. 5). In short, capital must be persuaded to flow back into Docklands by the injection of public money whilst the objective of and justification for this inflow is the provision of opportunities for making profits and the regeneration of London within the national economy.

Thus the objective is 'the critical imperative of maintaining London's role as the financial centre of the single European market' (King, 1990, p.152)

and, it must be added, of sustaining its role as a global centre of finance. The redevelopment of Docklands is not a mere consequence of inter-urban competition but an active player in the inter-urban game. And the game is fast and furious: by the year 2000, the Henley Centre (1990) predicts that competition to London will be severe, both from UK locations and from European cities seeking to attract business activity.

Although they do not perform the full range of global control functions, cities like Frankfurt, Zurich, Paris and Brussels compete effectively at a European level and represent a global threat to London in the longer term especially as the dynamics of European integration shift eastwards. Paris and Frankfurt have office rental levels one-half to two-thirds those of London in equivalent locations and top rents in both cities are more nearly those typical of London's Docklands (table 2.2). Of course, low rentals are a two-edged sword because high and growing rents push up the value of property, attract property capital and so help to sustain the supply of modern and purpose-built offices within a city and, thereby, its attractiveness to the activities which occupy these facilities. Low rents may attract low-order functions and help to repel funds for property investment. In the difficult circumstances of letting office space during a property slump, the developers of Canary Wharf have had to reconcile themselves to letting space to low-order office functions alongside the financial markets and corporate headquarters originally envisaged as the *raison d'être* of a development

Table 2.2   **Total occupancy cost of office space in major global cities** (£ per sq. ft; *c*. mid 1990)

Tokyo	110.25
London	
City	89.75
West End	89.50
City Fringe	46.00
Docklands	35.00
Paris	
City	52.25
La Défense	36.25
New York	
Midtown	45.00
Downtown	35.00
Frankfurt	37.00

Source: Salomon Brothers, Richard Ellis; in *Financial Times*, 21 September 1990.

which is still optimistically touted as 'London's third major business district' (Olympia & York, 1991).

With Canary Wharf, the scale of office redevelopment in Docklands is impressive – at least by the standards of London (chapter 6). Jones Lang Wootton point out that in 1992 office stock in the Isle of Dogs alone represents about 8 per cent of Central London's total office supply and could increase to 12.5 per cent by 1995 (Docklands as a whole will account for about 15 per cent) so that the area will be a major influence in the Central London office market. The development of Canary Wharf took place alongside a reduction in planning constraints within the City of London, so stimulating an expansion of office provision at a variety of sites. This fed the oversupply of total floorspace, thereby contributing to the fall in City rental levels and property values during the late 1980s and early 1990s (chapter 6).

Clearly, *inter*-urban competition is promoting the radical restructuring of urban space and generating *intra*-urban competition between localities in the attempt to cash in on sustaining London as a world city of finance. A recent survey of the London office market has made exactly the same point. Arguing that the City of London has lost its status as London's Central Business District, the survey goes on to applaud this development in suggesting that the 'new London has become competitive with the continent by providing modern office accommodation at lower costs . . . London's increasing ability to provide such alternatives will reinforce its dominance as a global city' (Byrne and Kostin, 1990, p. 16) .

But such a view places undue stress on the direct significance of the flows and stocks of capital in the built environment of London. And yet the evidence of both practitioners and academic analysts indicates that it is the functioning of markets and the regulations surrounding their operation rather than the buildings in which they take place which matter most in establishing and sustaining the competitive ability of a financial centre. Thus, its large share of international banking, foreign exchange dealing and the trading of foreign equities, as well as the number of foreign companies listed on the Stock Exchange, endowed London not only with global status but with a globally competitive edge. More recently, however, moves towards the harmonisation of financial services in the EC and the potential

eastward shift of the financial centre of gravity in Europe with the rapidly growing market in Deutschmarks (D-Mark) pose a threat to the future of London as Europe's pre-eminent financial centre.

In such a context, property developments in Docklands and elsewhere in London which mark little more than an admittedly impressive upgrading of the built environment are marginal in sustaining the competitive ability of London. The ready availability of what is perhaps the most modern range of vacant office space and dealing floors in Europe – most especially at Canary Wharf – as a result of the property boom of the late 1980s may help sustain the relative attractiveness of London, at least at the margins of inter-urban competition within Europe. But it is London's competitiveness as a set of markets that will determine its future role.

Conclusion

If the redevelopment of Docklands in the 1980s has failed to make a significant contribution to the global competitive position of London and if it has led to only partial redevelopment of the area, how should we assess the transformation within the region? The argument presented here is that the transformation of the Docklands is not due to what the DCC (1990, p. 6) call 'the peculiar Docklands factor': it is all rather more prosaic than that. Whilst in some senses – for example, the pace and character of change – the Docklands may be considered to be exceptional, redevelopment cannot be understood except in relation to the wider processes of economic and social change both nationally and internationally. The redevelopment of the region is a function partly of its location next to one of the three great cities of contemporary global capitalism at a time of rapid, if short-lived and qualitatively distinct, economic growth and partly of the ability of capital to lever so much public money out of the state in supporting its investments.

In short, change in Docklands is a product of processes only partly connected with the activities of the LDDC or the appropriateness of liberal policies towards the redevelopment of the inner city. The 'peculiar Docklands factor' is, in reality, little more than the public subsidy aimed at the reincorporation of Docklands into the global economy.

3 The LDDC's policy aims and methods

John Hall

The London Docklands Development Corporation has now passed its tenth birthday and is contemplating its own 'exit strategy' – institutional euthanasia. Inevitably, commentators will be drawn to the events of the most recent period, and especially the combination of market sluggishness and downturn since 1988 and seeming managerial vacillation during the same period. They will tend to overlook the remarkable turnaround in the *developability* of Docklands that was forged in the early years of the 1980s. In this chapter, I pay particular attention to the dominant philosophy of the early 1980s, and do this by mentioning some of the key actors in what, at the time, bore passing resemblance to theatrical improvisation. For the turnaround in the fortunes of 21 square kilometres or so of the London Docklands was achieved without a clear master plan like the London Docklands Strategic Plan of 1976 which clearly depicted a desired end-state.

Urban Development Corporations

The first systematic study of Docklands was that commissioned by Mr Peter Walker while Secretary of State for the Environment in 1971. The Greater London Council and the Department of the Environment jointly sponsored a study of the potential for the rebuilding of the Port of London Authority's upper docks between the Tower of London and Barking Reach. These docks were fast becoming idle reservoirs rather than the bustling waterside conveyors for a trading nation's imports and exports. The study was published in 1973, and offered five pictures of Docklands future (for the early history of Docklands planning see Brownill, 1990, chapter 2). Each was a phased and costed amalgam of the various ways of restructuring what was now being called the 'London Docklands' – the term was not in common use until Peter Walker's study was announced.

In broad terms, the five variants all required enormous levels of public investment in infrastructure (roads, railways, new Thames crossings, selective dock infill, public utilities) which would exceed private investment by a ratio of up to five to one. Attention was given to the question of how such investment was to be co-ordinated, and whether a special development authority would be appropriate. In fact Parliament began considering the question of management in 1974–75 and again in 1978–79, but each time its deliberations were overtaken by the calling of a general election. During the middle and later 1970s the managerial answer was the creation of the Docklands Joint Committee (DJC), a tri-partite body comprising eight GLC councillors, eight borough councillors from Tower Hamlets, Newham and Southwark (two each), and Lewisham and Greenwich (one each), and eight of the Environment Secretary's nominees. As it happened, all of these were Labour-controlled areas between 1974 and 1977 (fig. 3.1). Through the medium of a related land board, the DJC sought to execute its operational programme for the Docklands area, by which strategic aims enshrined in the 1976 plan were translated into who was responsible for making which site ready for development during a specified financial year.

It was not surprising that progress failed to keep up with intentions. Public spending was being squeezed as Britain applied to the International Monetary Fund for support. Docklands looked likely to have to endure a lingering redevelopment, beginning with the more favoured sites in Wapping and the south bank Surrey Docks zone which was always less fashionable despite being the same distance from the City of London. The West India and Millwall docks in Tower Hamlets and the Royals in Newham were to continue in operation until 1980–81.

In many ways 1979 has to be likened to a major geological event: the agent of change was the new Conservative Prime Minister, Mrs Margaret Thatcher, and her supporters, including Mr Michael Heseltine as Secretary of State for the Environment. In the Heseltine view, Docklands so far was a clear failure. Plans were not going to be realised. The public sector could not fulfil its promises. The sense of vision had been lost with the growing financial penury. Indeed, why was municipal and central government enterprise valued so highly in the regeneration effort?

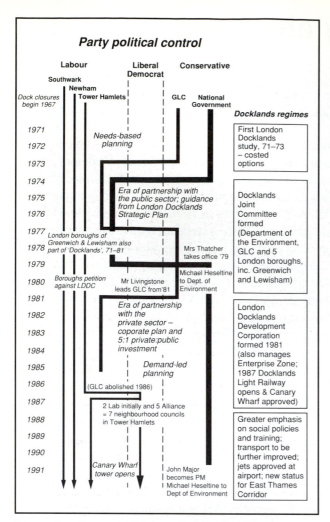

Figure 3.1 Party politics and planning initiatives in Docklands.

During the summer recess of 1979, Mr Heseltine announced that he would introduce legislation to allow the creation of Urban Development Corporations (UDCs), initially in the London Docklands and the Merseyside docks area. Whereas existing local authorities in these areas were multipurpose, UDCs would be single-minded development agencies, dedicated to achieving rapid regeneration in economic, employment and environmental terms. The proposed Liverpool UDC met with little opposition, but objections to the London proposals generated the longest sitting of the House of Lords in committee in recent memory. By summer 1981, a majority of five noble lords recommended the creation of the London Docklands Development Corporation and, soon after, the orders establishing the LDDC were confirmed.

In fact, the UDCs were a variant of the New Town Development Corporations (NTDCs) first established in 1946 to build Britain's post-war new towns. NTDCs had strong powers of land purchase, and drew up comprehensive master plans for creating 'balanced communities' in predominantly open countryside. In contrast, the LDDC was superimposed on a dense urban mosaic. Its objectives were to redevelop its area by investment in reclamation and infrastructure, together with business and community support for residential and commercial redevelopment.

As the debate about the LDDC in the House of Lords on 1 July 1981 made clear (House of Lords *Hansard* for that day), the government's case was principally that the scale and severity of the decline of Docklands created a problem of *national* rather than *local* importance (chapter 2). But the DJC, lacking development powers, could not implement its own strategic plan. Instead, a single-minded development corporation should reverse the decline by attracting new types of industry and private housing. This case outweighed that of the objectors who judged the proposed corporation to be undemocratic (replacing the elected local authority with the Environment Secretary's nominees – eleven apostles as one later to be appointed as such called them) and 'locally friendless'.

From concept to concrete

The LDDC can be viewed in the same terms as any firm or enterprise: to succeed it needed entrepreneurial talent, land, labour and capital. Three talented and energetic individuals established its direction and style. Its chairman, Mr (soon to be Sir) Nigel Broackes, was also the chairman of Trafalgar House, a highly diversified company that occupies many pages of the *Who owns whom* directory. Bob (later Lord) Mellish took the deputy chairmanship after a vigorous parliamentary career representing the dockers' constituency of Bermondsey, and the chief executive was the thrustful, and in many civil servants' eyes, unconventional, Reg Ward.

They were in the business of remaking images (chapter 4): transforming the view of Docklands from one of run-down unvisited docks to an area of opportunity almost on the very edge of the congested City of London. Once established, the LDDC used its treasury grant (some £60 million a year in its early years, nearly £300 million a year in the mid to late 1980s) first to buy land compulsorily, mainly from the Port of London Authority (PLA), then to make the land suitable for development, and finally to fund the necessary transport infrastructure. On an unprepossessing site

A docklands view a decade ago: note the high wall at the end of the street sealing off the dock. Photo: J M Hall

at Beckton on the edge of the far-east Royal Dock group four major house-builders agreed in 1981 to build some 600 houses for sale in an area where private housebuilding was unknown. They were built fast and sold equally quickly. Here was early proof of a latent demand for private investment at the most domestic level – family housing.

Another early coup was gaining approval for the construction of the Docklands Light Railway (essentially a modern tramway separate from the highway, and dramatically elevated across the West India Docks). The first stage would run from Tower Gateway, close to Tower Hill underground station, alongside the Fenchurch Street–Southend Line to Limehouse, and then snake through the Isle of Dogs to a terminus abandoned more than half a century earlier at Island Gardens opposite the Royal Naval College at Greenwich. Reg Ward knew that the perfect scheme would never get funding; equally he knew that a sub-optimal design could be upgraded if demand was proven later.

The unlocking of land and upgrading of transport was combined with obvious effect in the Isle of Dogs through the medium of the Enterprise Zone. Parentage of the idea in a British context is attributed to the geographer Peter Hall (Hall, 1988), and the then Chancellor of the Exchequer,

Sir Geoffrey Howe, contributed his blessing and Treasury funding. The notion was to designate most of the former PLA land on the Island and stretched around Leamouth to Canning Town, as an area in which for ten years from 1982 developers would be free from local business rates (to be paid to Tower Hamlets by the Treasury), free from many of the normal planning controls, and able to claim the costs of development in the zone against other taxable profits.

In fact the Island – with the Enterprise Zone at its core – became the geographical and symbolic or almost spiritual centre of the LDDC. The LDDC's main offices were established there, Limehouse Studios (for television production) became an early example of the desired new industries, a new red brick road (shades of the adventurers' yellow brick road in the 'Wizard of Oz'?) pierced the once forbidding dock walls, and in 1987 the Docklands Light Railway was running across the dock basins to do a workaday job in the most dramatic of visual settings.

Heron Quays, also in the Island, was the setting for another early experiment: bringing a Dash 7 aircraft (a quiet 60-or-so-seater turbo-prop) to land between the middle and main sections of the West India Dock. This was to prove the technical feasibility of bringing similar Short Take-Off and Landing aircraft into the chosen site in the Royals between the Royal Albert and King George V Docks. The London City Airport, like the DLR, also opened in 1987, was intended to be the catalyst for the Royals that the DLR was for the Island. But whereas the Island was soon to be settled by Canary Wharf, the Royals had to stand idly by during the late 1980s and early 1990s recession while the aircraft landed between abandoned docks and demolished warehouses and factories.

Such was the success of the initial Broackes–Mellish–Ward triumvirate and their small full-time staff – for many of the necessary skills of developers, surveyors, architects, engineers, marketing and public relations were contracted out to consultants – that the image and faces of Wapping, the Island and Surrey Docks were totally transformed by 1986. Land values escalated, such that the LDDC was able to anticipate making significant profits from sales of its acquired land. Already the hoped-for ratio of private to public investment of 5:1 was climbing towards 10:1.

Planning without a master plan

All of this was achieved by negotiation with private investors and the persuasion and cajoling of public authorities rather than by shading areas on a map. There were general planning briefs for particular areas – the supervision of regeneration was entrusted latterly to 'area teams' based in the highly distinctive parts of Docklands – but there was no overall master plan. Thus the break with the DJC's London Docklands Strategic Plan was complete: a willingness to capture any available development displaced the earlier desire for orderly and balanced development. *Demand-led planning,* a kind of courtship of private developers, had displaced *needs-based planning* in which there was to have been an arranged marriage between public authorities and somewhat reluctant developers.

It will be clear in chapter 5 of this volume that the process met with much local hostility, mainly from those who had supported the all-inclusive and socially and politically sensitive proposals of the London Docklands Strategic Plan. But the Broackes' team (and that of his successor, Sir Christopher Benson) were confident that they would succeed, and often appeared to relish confrontation with the old order. In answer to those asking the LDDC to put as much effort into community development as into physical regeneration, Nigel Broackes said: 'We are not a welfare association but a property-based organisation offering good value' (1982, quoted in Ambrose, 1986, p. 228). They coaxed the boroughs to their ways of thought, such that Tower Hamlets in the 1990s woos developers as if it had being doing so for decades, whereas in 1981 its officers had been instructed not even to *talk* with LDDC officials (Batley, 1989). Newham has remained somewhat purer, but now seeks to safeguard the public interest in what are expected to be largely privately funded developments in the Royals (London Borough of Newham, 1991). On the south bank, Southwark council has never sought the *grands projets,* and appears to satisfy more obviously local labour and housing markets in the Surrey Docks developments than those on the north bank, many of which are being promoted internationally.

Parliamentary scrutiny

The LDDC's methods, achievements and overall effectiveness as a policy instrument have been the subject of close scrutiny not just by local pressure groups, but also in parliament itself. The principal charge, made before the current economic down-turn, has been one of lop-sidedness: commercial considerations appeared to overshadow a broader interpretation of 'regeneration'.

A need for a better definition of regeneration by the DoE, and for the UDCs to establish clearer corporate planning objectives and monitoring of performance, was emphasised by the National Audit Office (1988). The NAO's strictures were echoed by the House of Commons Committee of Public Accounts (1988), which also underlined the need to secure effective working relationships with local authorities and other agencies, especially in support of education, training and social programmes. Concern had been expressed by the House of Commons Employment Committee (1988) about the apparent sluggishness of employment generation activities in comparison with physical regeneration.

Implementing – or even supporting – employment and social programmes causes real constitutional difficulties for the LDDC. It is not an education authority, a social services authority, an employment or training agency. The method chosen for assisting social and community development has been one of social infrastructure agreements with the three Docklands boroughs. An agreement was reached with Newham council in 1987, and a 'social accord' was signed with Tower Hamlets in 1989, principally to bring practical compensation for those adversely affected by the Limehouse Link and related road works. Social programmes in Southwark have also been supported. Unfortunately, the LDDC's own fuller appreciation of the timeliness of employment and social programmes (and its appointment of an energetic director of community affairs) has coincided with the property downturn. Likewise, hopes in the earlier 1980s that the benefits from regeneration would flow through the three boroughs as rateable income rose in the redeveloped wastelands were dashed as the government introduced a system of national business rates in 1990.

The replicability of the Docklands experience

Four new Urban Development Corporations were announced in 1987 (in Trafford Park, Greater

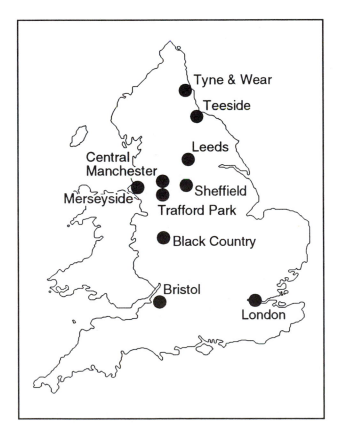

Figure 3.2 Urban Development Corporations in England.
Source: DCC (1990)

Manchester; the Black Country, West Midlands; Teesside; and Tyne & Wear), such that the London Docklands and Merseyside could now be regarded as 'first generation'. The first generation has been expected to complete its work in 10–15 years; the second generation has been told to take a decade. A 'third generation' established in 1988–89 (Central Manchester, Leeds, Sheffield, and Bristol) has been given 5–7 years. So there are now ten UDCs in England (fig. 3.2).

London overshadows all the others in its scale of expenditure (table 3.1, taken from the government's published annual expenditure plan), and in physical size. The expenditure figures relate mainly to exchequer grant-in-aid; again, they do not take account of tax-take foregone and the concentration of other government departments' spending in the area. The high LDDC figure for transport derives mainly from the Limehouse Link road (chapter 7). As a prototype, therefore, it is hardly typical of the rest. Being located in the capital, it has attracted media attention much more readily, and has been used by government ministers as a setting for 'photo-opportunities' and the launching of policy statements.

There are some other key differences. The London Docklands is an example not just of urban regeneration, but specifically of *waterfront* renewal. (This feature is also exploited to good effect elsewhere in the UK, including Belfast, Cardiff, Liverpool and Swansea, and even in inland Salford adjacent to the docks at the end of the Manchester ship canal.) The visual excitement for designers and capacity for image-makers and marketing people of what might be rather inelegantly called the land–water interface is evident from symposia on waterfronts (for example, US National Research Council, 1980; Hoyle *et al.*, 1988). And if you wish to see how urban designers can enhance the water's edge and manipulate vistas simply walk around the Canary Wharf development – too recent to appear in Nicholas Breach's photographs of a less-than-bustling Docklands of *c.* 1988 (Fishman *et al.*, 1990).

What is not to be doubted is the LDDC's capacity to deliver. Docklands 1991 is materially different from Docklands 1981. The corporation has accelerated physical renewal. The population has grown. New jobs have been located in the area. Road and railway construction is continuing at a pace unseen in London for over a century. 'London

Docklands' has become a shorthand for commentators on the culture and politics of the 1980s and 1990s who try to define Post-Modernism and the enterprise culture. I will not try to summarise all of this effort in a simple short phrase, but it is an effective monument to Michael Heseltine's stated 'single-minded determination' to regenerate the area. Unusually, Mr Heseltine had a second coming as Secretary of State for the Environment. A new type of dispersed linear city for the lower Thames caught his eye. Will this become an icon for the 1990s? What kinds of fiscal regime and political constitution will be created to foster growth in London's far-east channel funnel?

Table 3.1   **Grant aid to the Urban Development Corporations by the Department of the Environment, 1981/82 to 1990/91** (£ million)

UDC	Cumulative total since designation to 1990/91	1990/91
First generation designated (1981/82)		
London Docklands	1098.6	333.0
Merseyside	232.7	24.0
Second generation designated (1987/88)		
Black Country	95.4	32.0
Teesside	103.8	42.1
Trafford Park	63.5	24.2
Tyne & Wear	101.6	37.8
Third generation designated (1988/89)		
Bristol	18.7	13.4
Central Manchester	27.5	14.0
Leeds	25.5	14.0
Sheffield	36.5	19.0
Expenditure heads for the LDDC grant, 1990/91 (£ million):		
Land purchase, reclamation, environmental improvements	25.0	
Roads, transport, other infrastructure	244.0	
Housing and social facilities	37.5	
Assistance for private-sector development	0.3	
Administration, promotion, estate management	25.2	

Sources:

Grant to UDCs: *House of Commons Hansard,* Written Answers, 2 May 1991, cols 267–68

LDDC expenditure: *The government's expenditure plans 1990–91 to 1992–93,* HM Treasury 1990 (Cm 1008, HMSO)

4 Remaking the image of the Docklands

Darrel Crilley

Introduction

'We have no land use plan or grand design; our plans are essentially marketing images.' (Reg Ward, former Chief Executive of the LDDC, *The Times*, 18 November 1986).

As Reg Ward's comment suggests, transforming people's image of Docklands has been a crucial part of the whole redevelopment initiative. Just as cities such as Glasgow have advertised their attractiveness as cultural centres to attract tourists and relocating businesses, so too has the LDDC been acutely aware of the importance of packaging and selling whatever is unique to the locality. In fact, Docklands had to be marketed several times over: as a place to invest money, as a relocation site, as an integrated environment in which to live, work and play for a newer affluent generation of residents, and as a popular tourist destination. Faced with negative public perceptions of the Docklands as a wasteland of industrial decay and dereliction (despite the fact that 39,000 people lived in Docklands and there remained viable industrial enterprises), the LDDC recognised early on that to promote the area as a 'good business climate' and 'liveable city' it would have to persuade people to view the area through different lenses. As such the Corporation and allied property developers set out to project an image of a vibrant, rosy future in which the squalor of Docklands' former industrial landscape is seen to be cleansed and transformed into an alluring environment, albeit one with what is now sold as an enchanting nautical past. This forward-looking orientation is expressed in the numerous terms which have been used in the 1980s to advertise parts, or the whole of Docklands. It has been seen, for example, as a 'watercity of the 21st century', as 'the future close at hand', as a triumphant 'urban renaissance', as a 'mini-Manhattan', as the centre of a super new 'urban lifestyle', and sold by the LDDC as 'the most innovative and important urban regeneration project in the world'. Whatever the specifics of the image, Docklands is always portrayed as mini-city

unto itself, as an 'Emerging City', or more recently as the 'New Business City in the East'. This chapter looks at the resources and tools used to construct this new image of Docklands.

Direct marketing

The most deliberate attempts to give Docklands a new image have been two advertising campaigns funded by the LDDC, the first running in 1982–83, the second filling newspapers in 1990. They utilised a variety of media including roadside billboards, advertisements in national newspapers, TV advertisements and radio broadcasting. In straight financial terms, the first campaign was covered by a total of £31 million spent on promotion and publicity between 1981 and 1989, and the current, low-budget initiative extends to some £3 million. The second campaign does in fact follow a period in which publicity for the LDDC slipped down the list of financial priorities. As table 4.1 shows, relative to newer UDCs the LDDC did not allot great proportions of its budget to publicity, though the absolute amounts of money were large. At this time, also, private residential developers were busy mounting their own various marketing campaigns, represented in the selection in figure 4.1.

There were important differences between the two LDDC campaigns. Whereas the first was targeted mainly at the business community and intended to promote a basic awareness that the LDDC existed and that development and investment opportunities were available, and to give Docklands a clear identity as a place, the second campaign has been geared much more towards stressing the attractions of Docklands as a place to live and convincing people that Docklands has efficient transport services. This is evident if we compare figures 4.3 and 4.4 with some of the slogans used in the first campaign (fig. 4.2). In 1983, the attempt to promote Docklands depended on rational claims stressing its advantageous location ('Why move to

26

Figure 4.1 This advertisement collage shows the way in which developers were selling a 'lifestyle' as well as somewhere to live. The price reductions, however, indicate the collapse of the property boom by the late 1980s.

Figure 4.2 Some images intended to change the public perception of Docklands.

Table 4.1   Publicity and promotion as a percentage of total expenditure for UDCs 1988/90

UDC	1988/89	1989/90
London Docklands	1.2	0.9
Black Country	2.8	3.0
Central Manchester	17.2	7.3
Bristol	16.8	n.a.
Leeds	8.5	2.2
Merseyside	3.3	2.8
Sheffield	0.6	2.4
Teesside	8.2	5.9
Trafford	8.6	4.8
Tyne and Wear	7.1	5.8

Source: *Local Government Chronicle*, 1 September 1989

the middle of nowhere, when you can move to the middle of London?') and centrality ('How will you look to your clients if you move out of London?'). By contrast, the advertisements shown in figures 4.3 and 4.4 aim to convey the energetic richness and diversity which Docklands offers as a social environment relative to longer established residential areas in west London. Common to both

series of advertisements, however, was the 'branding' of Docklands as a unique place clearly differentiated from all others. In the first campaign this was attained by using material landmarks such as Tower Bridge as a form of corporate logo of Docklands and in the second campaign it is evident in the use made of the 'bend in the river' (made famous by the BBC programme *EastEnders*) as an easily recognisable sign of where Docklands is.

Heritage and the built environment

The built environment of Docklands has also been moulded with a view to establishing the right image for Docklands. The LDDC influences the appearance of the city in two main ways: through helping decide which style of architecture gets built; and through its responsibility for conservation of historic structures. On the first count the LDDC has clearly shown a preference for colourful, glitzy and unusual schemes, such as the Cascades building on the Isle of Dogs, which are capable of brightening up the urban scene and serving as identifiable Docklands landmarks. At the same time, Docklands has become an

Figures 4.3 and 4.4 Images intended to portray Docklands as an attractive residential environment on a par with other world cities; and with transport links to match.

acclaimed example of conservation-led redevelopment including at least 17 conservation areas and literally hundreds of listed structures from warehouses to churches. Following losses of historic structures through fire damage in the 1970s, the LDDC has operated a strict conservation policy, recognising that dock basins and warehouses were the key environmental resource of the area (chapter 11). Once sandblasted and safely converted to leisure and residential usage, this heritage gives Docklands its unique 'brand' image. Docklands is the London of Charles Dickens' novels and the use of historic names such as 'Old Bermondsey' or 'historic Limehouse' is encouraged. By the same token, restoration of open water spaces in Docklands has furnished an invaluable series of settings for new office buildings, leisure complexes and waterside housing that is unavailable elsewhere in London.

A spectacular and entertaining city

To create a festive, playful and entertaining feel that will lure visitors into Docklands a series of spectacular waterfront events has been staged. Most noteworthy of these was the 1988 Jean Michelle Jarre 'Destination Docklands' concert. Arranged in the derelict Royal Docks it was a Sight and Sound extravaganza intended as a celebration of the emerging information technology revolution and also as a means of placing Docklands firmly in the public eye (fig. 4.5). This crowd-pulling role was taken over on a regular basis by the London Docklands Arena on the Isle of Dogs, a mass entertainment venue that has drawn people down to the Isle of Dogs in thousands to witness both popular and classical performances ranging from Pink Floyd to Luciano Pavarotti. However, it is only too typical of the Docklands that the London Arena went into the hands of receivers in May 1991. Regeneration had itself become a spectacular event, especially as Canary Wharf's first stage neared completion: the tower itself was the setting for a spectacular laser show for New Year 1992. The area now ranks in the top three tourist attractions in London and there are 25 independent tour operators offering 'Seeing is Believing' trips of the area. The LDDC now runs its own rapidly expanding visitor centre offering an assortment of glossy brochures and videos telling of the achievements of regeneration. Added to this, the LDDC has frequently managed to enlist the support of royalty or prominent politicians by inviting them to open such developments as the

Docklands Light Railway in 1987, a feature seen by the Corporation to symbolise the spirit of arrival and breakthrough in the redevelopment of Docklands. Such 'royal seals of approval' are designed to enhance the public credibility of Docklands. The culmination of this attempt to inject a festive spirit was the 1990 London Docklands Festival, an eight-day spectacular of more than 166 events ranging from heritage tours through jazz concerts to circus activities. This is now scheduled to become an annual event designed to celebrate the redevelopment of Docklands.

A city of culture

Similarly, though yet to take effect, the LDDC launched an arts strategy in 1990 entitled 'Creating a Real City' which is strongly motivated by the desire to counter views of Docklands as a wasteland without cultural venues. Drawing lessons from examples such as the popular use of the Tate Gallery of the North in Liverpool's Albert Dock, a range of artistic exhibitions, events and venues are planned if finance is forthcoming. Although some private initiatives have already taken effect, the most notable being the Design Museum which has put its sponsor's development – Butlers Wharf – on the map (though it too has fallen on hard financial times), a broader range of initiatives may take effect. These encompass street theatre, open-air artists' studios, and everything from commissioning public art and sculpture (as in the case of Canary Wharf) to improve the visual qualities of the built environment to trying to attract a major national institution such as the National Portrait Gallery to move its premises to the Docklands. This, it is hoped, will provide continuous cultural animation for the area and raise people's expectations of the 'quality of life' to be obtained by living in Docklands. This new-found concern for the arts as an essential ingredient in 'regeneration' is not sentimental. Like roads, arts facilities are now seen as a highly productive 'soft infrastructure' which plays an increasingly important role in persuading the managers and personnel of national or international corporations to set up business in Docklands. So, though arts provision also has economic motives – to expand and diversify the employment base of Docklands for example – it is really used as a symbol of a thriving, living city conveying the 'can do' attitude towards redevelopment of inner-city areas.

Figure 4.5   Creating an urban spectacle: Jean Michel Jarre's 'Destination Docklands' concert, 1988.

The new East End? Outdoor life at Canary Wharf.

Myth or reality?

Great effort has therefore been devoted to promoting a catchy image for Docklands. But opinion is deeply divided as to whether the image-making was necessary or successful. Supporters will point to the positive effects that the early advertising campaign had on the decision-making of company executives in the print industry which has moved from Fleet Street to Docklands, and draw attention to the high profile Docklands now has compared to five years ago. A recent press release from the LDDC, for instance, claims to have transformed perceptions of the area as the 'backyard of London' to the 'front door of London'. Given that the advertisements in figures 4.2 and 4.3 were prompted by the poor image of Docklands being promoted in the national newspapers, such claims must be treated with caution. Against this, sceptics will emphasise that advertising and publicity is a frivolous diversion of funds from tackling pressing social problems and that they are just one more sign of disregard for local interests and views of Docklands (see the work of the Docklands Community Poster Project, chapter 5). They argue, moreover, that the preoccupation with image and identity is a covering gloss for real inadequacies in the planning and functioning of Docklands that cannot be rectified by pouring money into advertisements. Beautiful cities with waterscapes, art and a carnivalesque atmosphere can compensate only partially for real gains in employment and housing. To convince people of the viability of Docklands, so the argument runs, you must demonstrate the tangible benefits that lie behind the image.

Photo: LDDC

New housing in Docklands at the water's edge. The image of leisure, in this case sailing, was an important part of marketing campaigns.

5 Local resistance to the LDDC: community attitudes and action

Gillian Rose

Introduction

Ever since its inception, the LDDC has faced fierce opposition from local community groups. This chapter describes that opposition, and tries to explain its origins and estimate its effects on the way the LDDC operates. The first section describes the recent history of community organisations in the Docklands area and looks at the objections these groups make to the policies of the LDDC on issues like housing, transport, jobs and education. It also explores their alternative suggestions for the development of Docklands. These alternatives rest on a set of ideas very different from those of the LDDC: homes not offices, people before profit, people not land. The second section examines the priorities of local people in some detail, by looking at the products of various community arts groups and by listening to the voices of some local people. The final section assesses the impact of these protests on the LDDC by looking at events since the late 1980s.

The organisations of the local community

Who are they?

There are many groups in the Docklands area which represent local people. Some are statutory authorities, like the Greater London Council (GLC) before its abolition in 1986, and the local councils: the London boroughs of Newham, Southwark and Tower Hamlets. Many are non-statutory local bodies. Some of these, like the organisation for tenants on each council housing estate, or the Beckton Residents Group, exist to express the views of people living in a particular place. Others represent a group of people with particular interests, like the Wapping Parents Organisation and the Docklands Childcare Campaign. Some are highly organised, with paid workers and publications; others are much more informal. Given this variety, this chapter concentrates on just a few of the more prominent local organisations concerned with development in Docklands.

Many of the smaller groups affiliate to an area-based umbrella organisation: the Association of Island Communities, for example, or the North Southwark Community Development Group. Many of these are in turn affiliated to umbrella groups concerned with development issues. The oldest of these is the Docklands Forum (fig. 5.1). This originated in 1974, in response to the debates of the early 1970s over planning development in the Docklands area. Its membership of over 80 groups covers all Docklands and includes representatives of local community groups,

---

FUNCTIONS OF THE DOCKLANDS FORUM

The Docklands Forum aims to provide:

1. A voice of local communities in the planning and redevelopment of their area, particularly with regard to strategic issues

2. A research and information distribution facility for member groups and other local organisations

3. A focus for discussing and promoting the work of member groups and other local organisations and an information exchange

4. A platform for developing and pushing common action on Docklands issues, eg via public enquiries, petitioning Parliamentary bills and giving evidence to Parliamentary Committees

5. A means of access for local groups to regional, national and statutory bodies and to their decision-making processes

6. A means to achieve collective representation on other bodies, eg Skillnet Policy Board, DLR Consultative Committee

7. A means to co-ordinate liaison and consultation with the LDDC and developers in Docklands and to gain access to information and decision-making on development in Docklands

8. A channel through which to express members' views to the media and to promote public debate about the redevelopment of Docklands

9. An information source on Docklands for outside bodies and individuals, eg colleges and students

10. A lobbying point for local communities to promote their needs and to achieve significant gains fom the redevelopment of Docklands

11. A vehicle for promoting equal opportunities in Docklands

Figure 5.1 The role of the Docklands Forum

pressure groups like Tower Hamlets Action for Racial Equality, trade unions and trade councils, colleges, the London Chamber of Commerce, local churches like the Poplar Methodist Mission, environmental groups like Allotments for the Future and arts groups such as the Tower Hamlets Arts Project. It holds monthly meetings which discuss policies concerning development in Docklands and it tries hard to maintain a consensus among its members. It is seen as less extreme than some of the other local organisations.

The Joint Docklands Action Group (JDAG) is another important umbrella organisation, established in 1973. Like the Forum, it has a wide membership and functions as a resource centre for local opposition to the LDDC. Closely associated with JDAG is the Campaign to Restore Democracy in Docklands (CRDD), founded in 1981 by local groups involved in the House of Lords debate over the founding of the LDDC. CRDD has members from trade unions, Labour Party wards, churches, amenity groups and so on.

Both JDAG and the Forum, as well as councillors from the Docklands boroughs (and the GLC before 1986), are represented on the Docklands Consultative Committee (DCC), the final organisation in this complex network of local activity and protest. The DCC was set up by the Popular Planning Unit of the Labour-controlled GLC in 1982, to formulate an alternative plan for development in Docklands.

How are they funded?
These groups raise money in many different ways, from jumble sales to subscriptions to receiving grants from their local borough council. Before its abolition, some, like the DCC, CRDD and JDAG, were also funded by the GLC; afterwards, they were funded by local councils, until 1988 when JDAG and CRDD both lost all their funding. The future of the DCC is also in doubt.

Some organisations accept money from the LDDC. Not surprisingly, this is very controversial; those most vehemently opposed to the LDDC refuse to have anything to do with it. Some groups, however, especially since the abolition of the GLC and the increasing difficulty in finding finance in an era of continuing government cutbacks in public spending, have no choice but to accept LDDC cash. Over half of the Docklands Forum budget comes from the LDDC; the Forum recognises that the LDDC exists and won't go away, that it has

money it wants to spend (for whatever dubious reasons) on the local community, and that the Forum can use those funds to pay for its continued criticism of the LDDC.

What do they think about the LDDC?
The LDDC is based on the idea of private investment in development, and local groups argue this market-led approach is helping neither local people nor local industry. Criticism from many local organisations focused on two main areas: the type of development facilitated by the LDDC, and the way the LDDC is run as an organisation.

Local people are suffering because they cannot afford the new and expensive housing being built in Docklands. 'All the riverside is being gobbled up with luxury development – it's a public scandal. They've put the boot in,' says Maureen Davies of the Wapping Parents Action Group (fig. 5.2). Local industry is being squeezed out to make way for companies which employ very few local people. In the words of Terry Sullivan, a worker on a project to develop an alternative economic strategy for Docklands, 'the LDDC have no consideration for local people's needs – such as women's employment, ethnic minorities, disabled people and the young . . . the LDDC will continue to ignore them'. Above all, local people bitterly resented the lack of accountability of the LDDC. Unelected, meeting in secret, its consultations with

Figure 5.2   Cartoon from Greater London Council.
Source: GLC (1983)

the local community were seen as a farce. A worker for Southwark Council for Voluntary Services summed up local feeling when she said that 'you can't see the process – they're a law unto themselves . . . the power's all in their hands' (CRDD, 1983).

Community groups in Docklands wanted to see the area developed and improved as much as the LDDC does. But they wanted to see it improved for local people whose lives were centred on the district. Lil Hope of the Newham Docklands Forum said, 'what we want to see in the future is things being run by people who live in the area, so that when activities flourish it is local people who benefit' (CRDD, 1983). Many groups took as the starting point of their alternative vision of Docklands development the 1976 London Strategic Plan; the Forum was closely involved in its final version. Its aim was to reduce the deficiencies in housing, employment, communications and community services in the Docklands area by developing the large areas of land left empty by the closure of the docks. It stressed public investment, a contrast to the LDDC unanimously approved of among Dockland community groups. In 1984, all the different Dockland groups came together to write the People's Charter for Docklands, and they made five basic demands:

- full participation in our future
- housing to meet local needs
- jobs for local people using existing skills, and training for jobs in new industries
- improved local transport, both public and private
- improved essential services, like health and education

As for the statutory authorities, the GLC and Newham council were hostile to the LDDC from the beginning, and Southwark council joined them after the 1982 local elections. All these authorities were Labour-controlled; Tower Hamlets, with a Liberal majority, was more conciliatory. The attitudes of councils changed, though, in the late 1980s.

What do they do?
Local groups hold regular meetings to formulate policy and let the LDDC know what their feelings are. Occasionally they sponsor surveys of local housing or businesses and the extent to which local needs are being met by LDDC-sponsored developments. Given the perceived unresponsiveness of

the Corporation, however, many resorted to more unorthodox methods to get their message across.

Local community organisations have been endlessly inventive in their methods of protest. They have strung banners across roads and occupied luxury residential developments to protest at their cost; they have sat down in roads to complain about road-widening schemes near schools; a group of schoolchildren in Southwark devised a play to protest at the commercial development of Elephant Lane; and all this has received extensive media coverage, both local and national. Until the mid 1980s, JDAG produced for the CRDD a newsletter called Docklands Action News which was full of stories and jokes at the expense of the LDDC; it was especially good at tracing the connections between members of the LDDC Board and property companies hoping to develop Docklands. The DCC now produces *The Docklander* with similar verve (fig. 5.4), and the Forum also produces a regular newsletter. LDDC events at their offices on the Isle of Dogs have often been greeted by local people holding banners demanding cheap housing or LDDC accountability, accompanied by what a local newspaper describes as 'the Islanders' sing-along calypso anthem' 'Give Us Back Our Land' blaring out from loudspeakers.

Photo: The Art of Change

Figure 5.3   Graffiti in Bermondsey.

Figure 5.4 Front cover of *The Docklander* October/November 1988, from the Docklands Consultative Committee

There have also been large-scale demonstrations. The People's Armada was probably the most spectacular; this was a flotilla of ships, each carrying a group's representatives, that sailed in brilliant sunshine from North Woolwich to Westminster in 1984 (and again in 1985 and 1986; fig. 5.6). It delivered the People's Charter to 10 Downing Street, after being received by Ken Livingstone, leader of the GLC, in Jubilee Gardens.

The Royals complex of docks in Newham has prompted some of the most sustained campaigning by local people. In 1982 the LDDC proposed a Short Take-Off and Landing airport (STOLport) there. The immediate local response was the Campaign Against the Airport, for if built the runway would be only 40 metres from some people's back gardens. JDAG supported Newham Docklands Forum in the production of the People's Plan for Newham, which offered an alternative plan for the redevelopment of all the Royals. After local people had been fully consulted by JDAG opening an office in the area, contacting local groups, writing newsletters, establishing working groups and convening public meetings, in 1983 the Plan advocated the partial re-opening of the docks as well as the support of local and new high-tech

firms to increase local employment; it also suggested cheap housing, new public transport links, and childcare and play facilities. Not surprisingly, given the ethos of the LDDC, who controlled land-use in the Royals, these proposals, which required extensive public subsidy, were thrown out in a public inquiry in 1983.

The development policies of the LDDC have clearly come under concerted attack from local people. They have claimed that those policies are not improving life for the long-standing residents of the area; their experience of continued poor housing, lack of jobs and training and inadequate school and hospital provision makes them very sceptical about claims that the LDDC is a success. They have detailed ideas about an alternative strategy. But that alternative is not based on the profit motive of the LDDC; it is informed by a different set of values and priorities. The next section looks at these in more detail.

The oppositional culture of London Docklands

In order to understand the kinds of protest movements described in the previous section, local people's continued experience of deprivation is

Figure 5.5   Lobbying a board meeting of the LDDC, 1986.   Photo: The Art of Change

Figure 5.6   The People's Armada, 1984.

clearly a crucial factor; it has angered them into protest. Equally important however are the shared ideas through which they have articulated their protest. While the LDDC sees Docklands purely in commercial terms, local groups see Docklands very differently, through a different set of values. They voice their opposition to the LDDC not in monetary terms but by prioritising the rights of an established community to remain in its home. This gives their resistance to the LDDC a distinctive character.

Local community groups use a series of related concepts to make their case to the LDDC, and this section simplifies their very complex set of ideas by looking at just four of them: community, history, land and protest. The section looks at these motivating ideas by examining what local activists say about their campaigns, and also by studying the works of local community arts groups. These arts groups are usually resource centres who try to let local people articulate their own feelings by providing them with equipment and training in basic skills; many of them are affiliated to the Docklands Forum. The Docklands Community Poster Project, for example, has representatives of local community groups sitting on its collective, and decisions about their productions are made by

everyone on the collective, not just the practising artists.

Community

A sense of community is very important to local protest against the LDDC. Community implies a harmonious and united group of people centred in a particular place.

The idea of community often appears in people's memories of what life used to be like in riverside London before its first round of redevelopment after the Second World War. The interviews with elderly residents of the Isle of Dogs by members of the Island History Trust show the Island as a cohesive community of friendly neighbours. This sense of community was created in three ways. Firstly, families tended to live close together in inter-war east London, and the emotional ties of family life contributed to a sense of community; secondly, people often worked in the same neighbourhood as they lived, so they met the same people at work and in the local shops and pubs, and this too gave a feeling of cohesion to social life; and, thirdly, the poverty of the East End forced people to help each other out in bad times. The worker with the Island History Trust, Eve Hostettler, believes that this retrieval of a past communal identity encourages a renewed sense of community in the present, because history is central to local people's sense of themselves (figs. 5.7 and 5.8). In contemporary protests, the sense of community is important because it gives a feeling of solidarity and co-operation against outsiders, particularly the LDDC.

'Community' is empowering, then, but as an emotive word around which people mobilise it may also have some disadvantages. Its strong sense of solidarity can gloss over some inequalities within 'the community', as some of the women found out in their involvement in the People's Plan for Newham (Brownill, 1990). Neighbourhood communities are traditionally sustained by women who do not go out to work for wages, and ideas that a woman's role is not in the workplace and that the workplace as the place important to men is the most important thing to think about in planning, surfaced in the lack of regard sometimes shown by men to women's concerns expressed in the Plan.

It is also important to note that a tight sense of community implies solidarity among insiders but also the exclusion of outsiders. The different community groups along the river see themselves as distinct from each other, and are based on discrete social groups; 'Docklands' is a place name which came into being only recently. The 1984 Armada was in fact the first anti-LDDC event in which all riverside communities participated. This sense of belonging to a distinct and small-scale community may have weakened their potential impact on the LDDC by dividing the opposition into fragments. Further, very few of these groups have managed to involve ethnic minorities in their activities (a current concern of the Forum); East End communities are hardly ever racially mixed.

History
The fact that a sense of history is important to people in Docklands has already been mentioned. It gives them an identity and a feeling of belonging; they were in Docklands long before the LDDC. They argue that their historical presence gives them rights in the area, rights which the LDDC are ignoring. The Association of Wapping Organisations complained in 1983 that LDDC take-overs of council land were 'robbing the people of their heritage,' and the poem by East Ender Bernie Steer expresses this sense of injustice (fig. 5.9).

As well as claiming that the length of time local people have been living in Docklands gives them the right to have their needs respected, local groups

Figure 5.7   1935 Jubilee party in Strattondale Street, Isle of Dogs.   Photo: Island History Trust

Figure 5.8   An annual dinner at McDougall's flour mill, some time in the 1920s.   Photo: Island History Trust

DOCKLAND

Cranes standing still, no work for them
No movement, a monument to times past.
Silhouette outlined against a London sky.

Their reflection, mirrored in the waters
of a silent dock
Casting their shadows across the decks
of pleasure yachts.

Like a cancer spreading, with unchecked speed,
Wharves, warehouses closed overnight
Transformed, renovated
Not for people who have no place to live,
But for those who with obscene ease
Sail their yachts whenever they please,
Leaving them moored outside their second
homes.
It's all part of our social disease.

Docks closed
Once where dock workers played their part,
Shifting cargo, keeping London alive.
Now silence reigns, it is supreme,
thrusting aside this industrial scene.

Gone now, this way of life,
Testimony to the power of those few,
Whose decisions carry far and wide,
Eroding, encroaching, changing the
Character of our riverside.

Figure 5.9 Poem by East Ender Bernie Steer.

also suggest that the kinds of things their parents and grandparents and great-grandparents did in the past are significant to their present-day struggles. They remember particular historical events, celebrate them and use these to construct a tradition in Docklands – a tradition of local solidarity and resistance to outsiders.

Many local groups tell a story of Docklands' past which stresses the struggles of ordinary people to improve their lives. A recent video called *East of the City* is a very good example of this. It discusses the Fascist anti-semitism of the 1930s and the National Front racism of the 1970s and 1980s and the forms of protest each provoked from ordinary east Londoners, particularly the famous Battle of Cable Street in 1936 when thousands turned out to prevent Oswald Mosley marching his Blackshirts through the streets of Stepney (fig. 5.10). The video also describes dockers' strikes for better pay and job security, and rent strikes in the 1930s for better housing conditions. Another video, *Fly a Flag for Poplar*, made by local people, remembers the events of 1921 when the members of Poplar Borough Council were sent to prison for spending too much money on the relief of the local poor (fig. 5.11).

These videos remind people of their previous struggles and give them courage to fight the LDDC.

Land

Docklanders have a fierce attachment to particular places in the Dockland area. The song 'Give Us Back Our Land' insists that 'this land is our land', and North Southwark Community Development Group claim that the LDDC 'has stolen our land'.

The Elephant Lane Young People's Theatre Group said at the time of the People's Charter in 1984 that the site they came together to defend 'holds great sentimental value in the area and local people are asking that the land be redeveloped for their benefit'. The emotional resonance certain places like Elephant Lane has is not surprising. The work, community and family lives of local people centred around them and their disappearance creates a painful sense of loss. The Island History Trust has made a travelling exhibition about Burrell's paint works on the Isle of Dogs, which tells of the sadness and anger of local people at its closure. This grief is a strong emotional source of protest against the LDDC, for in the place of

beloved local landmarks are rising new industries which have no place for locals, except as the most marginalised workers: cleaners, caterers. Some local arts groups work with this sense of belonging to a place, and use the landscape which people see every day to campaign against the LDDC. The Docklands Community Poster Project erects large photomurals in pedestrian streets, and changes their images over time to reveal the processes of LDDC exploitation (fig. 5.12).

Collective protest

This is the final theme which structures local protest against the LDDC. I have already noted that past protests are remembered; but they are recalled in a specific way. Although leaders and particular individuals always appear, the stress is on all local people working together for change. *Fly a Flag for Poplar* demonstrates this. It shows local people meeting, organising a fair, then campaigning for a community centre which they eventually win. The film emphasises the collective action necessary to win better conditions for themselves.

These four themes – community, history, land and collective protest – are some of the central values

Figure 5.10   The Battle of Cable Street.   Photo: Tower Hamlets Local History Library

Photo: Tower Hamlets Local History Library

Figure 5.11   Poplar councillor George Lansbury with colleagues and supporters, 1921.

of local community groups campaigning against the LDDC. They produce the message that local people matter and that communities are more important than profits. In the words of Pat Henshaw of the Association of Island Communities, 'Docklands is about people. If the LDDC are allowed to continue it will kill off the communities, it will destroy the people.'

Have these protests made any difference to the LDDC?

Protest against the LDDC has continued for nearly a decade and has certainly influenced LDDC policy and operation. This section examines the extent of its impact, although it should be noted that such change as there has been in LDDC policy and working is also attributable to the recommendations of the 1988 House of Commons Employment Committee and to developers' complaints to the LDDC about the difficulty of working with local people. Both expressed fears that the 'development' which has occurred in Docklands is threatened by the absence of social and environmental investment by the LDDC, so that the area looks a mess, has poor leisure, health

and transport amenities, and has a poorly educated and untrained workforce.

The policies of the LDDC in the late 1980s changed quite noticeably in a direction welcomed by community groups. In 1988 it set up a Community Services Division, and 1989 saw policy papers on health, social housing and childcare published by the LDDC, all of which acknowledged the needs of the local community. The late 1980s also witnessed the signing of Accords between the LDDC and the boroughs of Newham and Tower Hamlets. These provided some benefits for local people – like social housing, guaranteed numbers of local jobs, and grants to community projects – as part of large redevelopment schemes. Brownill (1990) thinks the promised social housing is perhaps the greatest benefit from the LDDC for local people.

However, local groups remain sceptical about the extent of the LDDC's change of heart. The Docklands Forum, for example, notes that despite the commitment to community health services in the LDDC health policy paper, Community Health Councils are not represented on the LDDC's Docklands Health Advisory Group. Commitments

Figure 5.12   The changing picture of Docklands.

Photo: The Art of Change

to social housing seem to be taking an inordinately long time to be implemented, and unemployment in the Docklands has remained virtually unchanged: 3,553 in July 1981, and 3,328 in January 1991. Moreover, old doubts about the LDDC's intentions hover over its recent attempts to become more open and accessible to local people. In August 1989 the LDDC produced and circulated a paper which acknowledged the extent of local suspicion and hostility towards itself; while it realised that commercial constraints and its obligations to satisfy the needs of developers were bound to produce continued conflict between itself and the local communities, it said it would like to improve consultation procedures particularly over issues raised again and again by local groups: health, education and training, transport, among other things. But the Forum commented that the LDDC often seemed to confuse giving information to local people with consulting them. Consultation implies listening to groups and responding to their input, not simply giving them glossy handouts telling them what the LDDC has decided.

Community groups like Forum, JDAG and the DCC remain convinced that the LDDC is an undemocratic body which should be abolished as soon as possible. And the LDDC, in its continued refusal to listen to and implement the wishes of local people, and in its recent decision to stop funding the Docklands Forum, seem to be proving them right.

In July 1991, on the tenth anniversary of the LDDC, community action groups organised a protest on the wharf opposite the expensive banqueting tent holding the LDDC's own celebration. They shouted their protests across the river, and one group, the South Poplar and Limehouse Action for Safe Housing (SPLASH), made a joke set of awards to parody those the LDDC were giving out. This demonstrates that, after a decade of regeneration LDDC-style, local community groups still feel the only prize the LDDC will ever win from them is the booby prize.

6   Land and property: the pattern and process of development from 1981

Andrew Church

The land issue in the 1970s

Control of the land market is central to the LDDC's regeneration strategy. The LDDC has been able to obtain land, clear and prepare the land, and then sell it off to the private sector. Previous organisations charged with the regeneration of Docklands found the issue of land to be one of their major stumbling blocks.

In the 1970s the GLC and the boroughs had obtained and prepared certain sites. The former London Docks and Surrey Docks were both filled in to provide development sites and Beckton marshes were drained. However, the Docklands Joint Committee established in 1974 found it hard to assemble the land required to implement its London Docklands Strategic Plan (chapter 3). Publicly controlled companies like the Port of London Authority, British Gas and British Rail were major landowners, but were unwilling to sell land cheaply, preferring to wait until values rose.

The Community Land Act of 1976 and the establishment of a Docklands Land Board in 1977 were to be the devices by which the Docklands Joint Committee built up a land bank. The Act failed to live up to expectations since land was often given a high value based on past or future uses that local government could not afford. This meant that the Docklands Land Board had purchased only three acres of land by 1980 (Brownill, 1990).

At the same time, the amount of vacant and derelict land was continuing to grow. The LDDC's area is 21 square kilometres, which is half the size of Cambridge and two-thirds the size of Oxford. By 1981, 40 per cent of Docklands was derelict or vacant. This led the LDDC to describe Docklands as a derelict desert, which was clearly an exaggeration since there were still almost 40,000 people living in Docklands along with firms employing 28,000 people. Nevertheless, the key problem as perceived by the LDDC was how to release the land available in Docklands.

The LDDC's approach to the land market

The 1980 Local Government Planning and Land Act gave the LDDC considerable powers and resources to acquire land. The LDDC has gained land in three ways. First, it uses its grant from government to purchase land on the open market. Second, it has used Compulsory Purchase Orders (CPOs) to force owners to sell land subject to compensation. Sometimes the threat of a CPO was enough to encourage owners to sell. Third, and most controversially, the Minister for the Environment is able to transfer land from one public authority to another subject to compensation. This process is known as 'vesting' and land was vested from the local authorities and given to the LDDC. Brownill (1990) notes that compensation paid to local authorities for vesting was often below the market value of the land. Furthermore, Tower Hamlets and Newham lost their major sites designated for new public housing. The LDDC can be seen as part of a wider central government strategy to reduce the planning power of local government. Vesting further erodes local authority control over redevelopment. Many of the local community groups opposed to the LDDC claimed that the LDDC's powers meant that a once and for all opportunity for local residents to influence the nature of land redevelopment was lost (see chapter 5 on this point).

Using these strong powers, the LDDC built up a considerable land bank. By March 1991, the LDDC had acquired 2,109 acres (20 per cent were water) which is over 40 per cent of the total area of Docklands. 401 acres were to remain as waterspace and 483 acres were to be used for infrastructure such as roads, the DLR and environmental improvements. This means that of the land acquired by the LDDC, 1,225 acres were available for development. By 1990, 661 acres had been sold on to the private sector and 564 acres (mainly in the Royal Docks area) were either being reclaimed or awaiting development.

May 1988

September 1990

November 1991

The Canary Wharf complex takes shape 1988–91.

Photos: Olympia & York

Newspaper headlines in May 1992 reveal the extent of the financial crisis which hit the Canary Wharf project and provoked widespread international publicity.

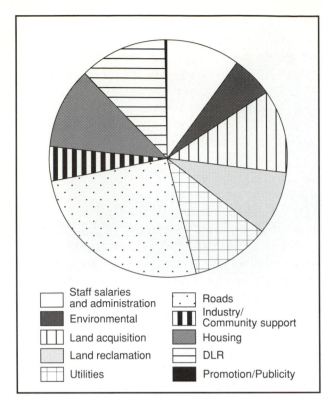

Figure 6.1   LDDC expenditure 1981–90.
Source: Parliamentary Answer, 2 May 1991

Not surprisingly, the LDDC has had to spend heavily on land: 77 per cent of money received from central government in the first five years of the LDDC's operation was spent on purchasing, reclaiming and environmentally improving land. This had fallen to 9 per cent of central government grant by 1990/91, so that overall for the decade between 1981 and 1991, 22 per cent of the LDDC grant was spent in this way (fig. 6.1). Control over land, coupled with the LDDC's incentives and planning approval powers, have allowed the LDDC to pursue an approach to regeneration that could best be described as market-led. The LDDC makes the land available and then allows private sector market forces to determine largely the nature and type of development on particular sites. However, it would be wrong to describe this approach as *laissez-faire*. Large-scale public expenditure on land and incentives was essential to attract the private sector.

Ambrose (1986) is highly critical of this whole approach, claiming that 'the LDDC has, in effect, expropriated land in large parcels and sold it on to builders at submarket prices'. Nigel Broackes, the first LDDC Chairman, took a different view claiming that the LDDC's strategy had started by 1984 to attract the interest of commercial property developers making 'Docklands part of the London property scene where previously it was a no-go area' (quoted in Ambrose 1986, p. 240).

The pattern of development and the land market since 1981

The scale of physical regeneration, in the form of new buildings, is seen by the LDDC as their major achievement since 1981. By 1991, 15 million square feet of commercial space had been constructed. The 1991 Corporate Plan suggested this figure would have risen to approximately 34.7 million square feet by mid 1995, which is greater than the city centres of Manchester and Birmingham combined. However, the recent property slump in Docklands may mean some of this space is not built on for many years. In the housing property market 15,000 new homes have been completed or begun (chapter 8). However, it is important to remember that the pace of redevelopment has been quite varied. It is possible to identify three phases in property development in Docklands in the 1980s.

Phase 1: 1981–85. Hi-tech, low-rise Docklands
In the early 1980s private-sector interest and development was very limited. In a period of recession the big institutional commercial property investors, like pension funds, viewed developments in Docklands as high-risk ventures. Consequently, some of the first commercial developments were undertaken by smaller property companies from the north of England, such as Ogden Estates who developed Indescon Court.

Many of the buildings constructed in this period were 'Hi-Tech' units of the type found on greenfield business parks in rural areas and the outskirts of major cities. The phrase 'Hi-Tech' is misleading since it refers to low-rise commercial units, some of which may be flexibly designed to allow either office or industrial/storage uses. The only office development in Docklands in this period occurred at established locations on the edge of the City of London that happened to fall within the LDDC area, such as London Bridge City on the south bank of the Thames between London and Tower Bridge.

The housing market expanded rather faster. By March 1985, 2,460 units had been completed and a further 4,600 were under construction (chapter 8). Many of the big names in British house building, such as Wimpey and Barratts, had invested in Docklands, often attracted by the cheap price of the land the LDDC was selling.

Despite the slow start to commercial redevelopment, land values had started to rise quite

Photo: LDDC

The new *Financial Times* building, with the Canary Wharf Tower.

sharply by 1984. The LDDC's Annual Report in 1984/85 showed that in general land values had risen fourfold since 1981. In the Enterprise Zone, land that had a minimal value in 1981 was selling at £80,000 per acre in 1984 and by the end of 1985 the price had leapt to £250,000 per acre. The Docklands land and property market was just about to take off in a manner never imagined in 1981.

Phase 2: 1985–88. The boom
National economic growth and the expansion in the City of London contributed to a marked increase in the demand for commercial property in London in the mid 1980s. Many commentators predicted this increase in demand would require considerable amounts of new development since central London's older offices would be unable to accommodate the computer systems and large open-plan offices needed in future. In addition, developers were finding it easier to raise money for new speculative developments. For example, foreign banks were prepared to lend considerable sums to property companies (chapter 2) and one estimate suggests that 43 per cent of the £37 billion in outstanding UK property loans is owed to overseas banks (Docklands Consultative Committee, 1991).

At the same time, the London housing market, which had been in the doldrums in the early 1980s,

Indescon Court: offices in the Enterprise Zone on the Isle of Dogs.

Photo: LDDC

Photo: LDDC

New buildings, often of very distinctive design. Isle of Dogs Neighbourhood Centre by Tehaik Chassay Architects.

began to heat up as rising personal incomes and the easier availability of mortgages combined with economic expansion to produce a marked increase in the demand for houses for sale. These pressures for growth perhaps affected Docklands more dramatically than any other part of London.

The subsequent office development boom in Docklands was centred on the Enterprise Zone due to the lucrative tax allowances for property development. In 1985, development started on medium-sized office blocks like South Quay Plaza. Shortly afterwards proposals appeared for the much larger Canary Wharf project. Initially the development was led by G. Ware Travelstead, an American property developer. When he was unable to raise adequate funding the Canadian property company Olympia & York, run by the Reichmann brothers, stepped in to continue the project. Canary Wharf is a 71-acre site on which there are plans for 12 million square feet of offices and 0.75 million square feet of shops and leisure facilities. A total of 24 to 26 buildings are planned and the first and part of the second phase of development containing 4.3 million square feet of offices was

completed by late 1991, with the remainder initially planned for completion by 1996. Prior to this the largest single development proposed in Britain was at London Bridge City on the edge of the City of London, which contained a mere 2 million square feet.

The Canary Wharf proposals had a dramatic effect on redevelopment in Docklands as they indicated that the area could become a major office centre. Crédit Suisse First Boston and Morgan Stanley International were two of the first financial companies who indicated they would be moving to Canary Wharf, partly because they had invested money in the development itself. Texaco, American Express and the advertising agency Ogilvy and Mather are other big names who initially agreed to occupy office space. The developers Olympia & York argued that Canary Wharf would be a location not for companies' back offices, but instead for their prestigious European headquarters.

In this period between 1985 and 1988 numerous office proposals were presented to the LDDC so that by 1991 the amount of office space in Docklands either planned, or under construction, or built between 1981 and 1991, totalled a staggering 47 million square feet (Docklands Consultative Committee, 1991). Some of this is only planned and may not be built for many years. However, this figure excludes the Royal Docks, where in 1987 three major development proposals were outstanding. These adjoining schemes aimed to construct over 9 million square feet of space including not only offices but also London's biggest shopping centre, a 20,500-seater stadium and a major hotel.

The housing market also boomed. In 1981 the LDDC had aimed to construct 13,000 housing units by 1991. The pace of development meant that in 1987 the LDDC revised its target to 25–30,000 by the end of the century (chapter 8). The price of land and property also rose sharply. By 1988 riverside housing sites were selling for £5 million per acre. However, the LDDC was still prepared to subsidise developers by selling land cheaply. In 1987, 20 acres of Canary Wharf was sold to

Olympia & York for £400,000 per acre despite the fact that other sites in the Enterprise Zone were selling for over £1 million per acre. Not surprisingly, house prices rocketed. In 1987 Tower Hamlets recorded a 38 per cent increase in house prices, well above the London average of 20 per cent (Brownill, 1990). In the commercial market, office rents doubled from under £10 per square foot at the end of 1985 to £20 per square foot at the end of 1987. Many developers and home owners made large speculative gains, but these boom years were soon to disappear.

Phase 3: 1989–92. The property slump
The construction of offices and houses still continues in Docklands, but at a much slower pace. All the indicators suggest the Docklands property market is very unhealthy. In 1990–91 a series of Docklands property companies were declared bankrupt. These included the developers of Burrells Wharf, South Quay Plaza, Tobacco Dock, Baltic Wharf and Butlers Wharf. As the demand for housing has disappeared so house prices have fallen, often as fast as they grew. Coupland (1989)

The atrium at 10 Cabot Square at Canary Wharf, part of the office complex.   Photo: Olympia & York

Photo: LDDC

Some of the jungle of buildings in the Enterprise Zone on the Isle of Dogs, with South Quay station in the foreground.

claimed that advertised prices at the Cascade riverside development for a two-bedroom flat rose from £109,000 in January 1987 to £193,000 in July 1988, only to fall to £128,000 by the end of 1989 (see also chapter 8). A number of housing developers now offer 50/50 deals which allow purchasers to buy a property at half price for five years and then purchase the remaining half at a later date.

Nearly half the office space in Docklands was vacant in early 1991, some office rents on the Isle of Dogs had fallen to around £15 per square foot and in March 1991 one office block was offering space at £10 per square foot (*Estates Times*, March 1991). By 1992 Canary Wharf itself became the most dramatic casualty of the property slump. Merril Lynch and the European Bank of Reconstruction and Development had preferred locations in the City of London to Canary Wharf. Saatchi and Saatchi, the advertising agency, were offered an incentive package of £30 million by Olympia & York, but even this was not sufficient inducement to move to Docklands. By April 1991, only just over half of the office space in the first phase of Canary Wharf had an occupier for the

opening in late 1991, and in early summer 1992 the Canary Wharf project was placed in administration (chapter 2). Further east the Royal Docks development proposals have all but collapsed. Two of the potential developers withdrew claiming that the price of the land was too high in a recession and the third developer had been refused a City Grant from central government that it had hoped would make the scheme profitable.

The reasons for the slump are complex. High interest rates that raise the cost of personal mortgages have hit the housing market. The slowdown in the national economy and rationalisation by firms in the City of London have certainly led to a fall in the demand for office space. However, a lack of demand is not the only problem facing the developers of office property in London. One analyst recently quoted in *The Financial Times* (29 October 1990) claimed that 'the main problem facing the property market is not high interest rates, or a lack of tenant demand but simply the huge volume of development work in progress'. London's office market problem is one of over-supply both now and in the future as more new offices currently under construction are completed. This problem is reflected in office vacancy rates in the City of London that rose from 9.4 per cent in July 1990 to nearly 15 per cent by spring 1991 (*Estates Times*, March 1991; and see also chapter 2). It is not just in Docklands that developers are unable to find occupiers for new offices, it is a London-wide problem.

The difficulties of the property market are not just the result of macro-economic forces. The role of planning authorities is also important. The LDDC's lack of restrictions in Docklands was partly responsible for the massive scale of office development in the area. The lack of planning control and the lack of a London-wide planning authority meant there was no strategic attempt to assess whether London needed all the office space. Furthermore, in about 1985 the City of London planning authority began to worry that its position as the leading location in Europe for financial sector firms would be harmed by competition from Docklands where rents were considerably lower. The City's response was to revise dramatically its 1984 plan that had been very restrictive on new development and relax its planning rules. This led to planning permission being granted for a further 20 million square feet of offices. The problems of letting office space in Docklands have been made worse by the transport problems and recent poor image of the area. An additional problem the LDDC has to face is that the property slump affects its expenditure plans. The LDDC is allowed to spend the money it gains from land sales. In 1985/86 this amounted to £10 million rising to £107 million in 1988/89, but then falling to £27 million in 1990/91. Between 1981 and 1990, 20 per cent of LDDC's income had come from land sales, but the recent decline has meant that the LDDC has had to reduce some of its planned expenditure on social projects.

Conclusions and the future

The slump in the property market in Docklands has slowed down the whole regeneration process. Some take a bleak view of the future of

development in Docklands. A report by the estate agents who advise London Regional Transport claimed that, apart from Canary Wharf, no new development would start in Docklands for six years (*Estates Times*, January 1991). Others tried initially to put on a brave face. Olympia & York tended to argue that the problems of development in Docklands were short term and that over a twenty-year period it would become a very successful office centre. Economic recovery in the 1990s and new transport links to Docklands would ensure the area's success. Indeed, Olympia & York claimed that Canary Wharf was doing London a favour. After 1992 and the establishment of the Single European Market, London would face strong competition from other European cities, particularly Paris and Frankfurt, as a location for financial services and the headquarters of multinational companies (chapter 2). Olympia & York claimed that the over-supply of office space would bring down rents in London to a competitive level and Canary Wharf would provide the high-quality prestige space that international firms require. However, the severe and much-publicised crisis which overcame the Canary Wharf project in 1992 made these optimistic predictions seem extremely unrealistic.

How long the property scene will be in the doldrums remains to be seen. What is clear, however, is that the LDDC's approach to the land market combined with the major financial incentives of cheap land and tax breaks in the Enterprise Zone have resulted in the redevelopment of considerable areas of derelict and vacant land. Equally, an unfettered approach to property development was partly responsible for the boom and slump of the Docklands property market, which creates new and formidable problems for the regeneration process in the 1990s.

Note
Except where stated all figures used in this chapter come from LDDC Annual Reports or Corporate Plans that can be obtained from the LDDC, Thames Quay, 191 Marsh Wall, London E14 9TJ.

7 Transport

John Hall

Introduction

London is a port city open by seaways to the rest of the world, but for most of its working life Docklands has been virtually cut off from the city surrounding it. This might appear an extreme statement, but consider the facts. The near-east upstream docks, the London and St Katharine and Surrey Commercial Docks, never had adequate connections to the railway network, although railway spurs did approach the warehouses to the north of St Katharine's Dock. A new road was built in the 1820s, Commercial Road, to connect the City of London with the East and West India Docks, but once off that road at either end any carter or haulier would be faced with a congested maze of inadequate local roads.

Things were hardly any better until the early 1980s. For example, a map of accessibility to rail passenger stations (Underground and British Rail) in Greater London in 1967 showed the Isle of Dogs and the Greenwich peninsula to be the worst provided areas of London so close to the central area. On numerous occasions throughout the 1970s I led excursions around Docklands, but without special dispensation was not able to take a coach behind the high dock walls: the docks were a fortified place, clearly visible on a map or from a tower block, but almost invisible from the surrounding streets.

So we can appreciate the immediate transport challenges facing the LDDC when it was established in 1981. It sought to open up its area to London, for the benefit of existing residents and businesses in the area, and of any person or goods interested in getting in to this largely unknown sector of the metropolis. Literally speaking, it wanted to put Docklands on the map, for all maps of 'central London' progressed no further east than the Tower of London. Transport developments rank highly in the image-makers' armoury, not least because the dotted lines on maps that show projected routes imply a commitment to expenditure. It has to be appreciated that the LDDC's ideas about how to do all of this would

not arise from thin air. Its own staff and its consultants would not start with a clean sheet; they would dust down all the various proposals made in the 1970s, if not before, and examine their validity as part of the new regeneration exercise.

Before examining the various options and proposals in greater detail, there are some important points to note about major transport developments. To begin with, there is now abundant evidence from the USA and western Europe that transport improvements themselves do not lead directly to economic development. In fact, opening up an area by new road or rail investment might often help residents and businesses to leave, more than help newcomers to enter. Yet transport developments are regarded, not least by politicians, as of considerable value in promoting positive images about an area, although in major urban areas of the size and complexity of London, selective transport improvements do little to change overall journey times or patterns. However, they can bring noticeable improvements in small areas. Further, major transport developments can be at least ten years in the making, with the construction time taking only a quarter or so of this time – it is the political and legal obstacles which account for most of the period taken.

Putting Docklands on the map, beginning with the Isle of Dogs

In chapter 3, the attention given by the LDDC to achieving early results on the Isle of Dogs was emphasised. The closure of the West India and Millwall Docks in the centre of the Island coincided with the LDDC's assumption of powers. One of the first major works undertaken by the corporation was the construction of a horse-shoe shaped road inside what had been the protective dock wall of the Port of London Authority. Road traffic was soon able to skirt the docks on the so-called 'red brick road', a new road which, unusually for London, was surfaced with red bricks laid in a herringbone pattern.

The road certainly eased traffic circulation within the Island, which earlier was brought almost to a standstill whenever the lift bridge at the entrance to the West India Docks was raised at high tide to allow vessels to pass to and from the Thames. The next step was to plug the Island into east London and indeed London as a whole. Various ways of doing this had been proposed over the years. Horace Cutler, Conservative leader of the GLC from 1977 to 1981, had wanted to see the Jubilee line of the Underground extended eastwards beyond Charing Cross and the Tower of London into Docklands and ultimately to Woolwich. There had also been discussion about a possible Docklands Southern Relief Road which would have traversed the Surrey Docks and Isle of Dogs on its way downstream. But the 1970s and early 1980s was not the time for gaining support for major public transport investment in London.

Nevertheless, for promotional as well as practical benefits, the LDDC wanted to connect the Island, and its Enterprise Zone, to the City of London. The means ultimately chosen was the Docklands Light Railway (DLR), which is really an urban tramway running on a separate track (figure 7.1). Its distinctive blue, red and white livery is now familiar to tourists and commuters alike on the twin branches from Tower Gateway/Bank and from Stratford, which converge at West India Quay before progressing the full length of the Isle of Dogs to Island Gardens opposite the Royal Naval College at Greenwich. It gained government approval as a low-cost scheme (less than £80 million) which made use of railway alignments abandoned in some cases 60 years or so earlier. It offers spectacular views across the dock basins on the Island, and less dramatic views of 1930s, 1950s and 1960s housing schemes shoehorned into the jumbled fabric of the Victorian city at Shadwell and Limehouse.

The DLR is criticised for being a 'toytown' railway: cheap, cheerful, colourful. Its stations are functional but rudimentary, its trains were short (single-unit until 1991), its fully automatic operation in the early years after opening in 1987 subject occasionally to irritating breakdowns and delays. (The embarrassing breakdowns that coincided with the opening of the Canary Wharf tower in summer 1991 must have had some part to play in the government's decision to take responsibility for the DLR away from London Transport and to give it to the LDDC and hence the Department of the Environment – not Transport.)

But the DLR would not have been approved unless it *had* been cheap. While on the drawing board from 1982 it was conceived as a means of carrying about 1,600 people an hour on each of the two branches. At this time, Canary Wharf looked likely to become an area of mixed light industrial uses within the Enterprise Zone, with its best-known occupant the Limehouse film studios.

But the anticipated scale of development was overturned by the announcement in 1985 that the Canary Wharf development consortium (Crédit Suisse First Boston Ltd, Morgan Stanley International, First Boston International and the Travelstead Group) intended to develop 12.5 million square feet (1.2 million square metres) on the wharf, employing up to 40,000 people directly, and with the addition of half that number of jobs generated elsewhere. How could the DLR possibly cope with that level of travel demand focused on an area of only 71 acres (21 acres of wharf, measuring 380 feet by 2,500 feet, 25 acres of buildings above the existing water, and 25 acres further between the wharf and the River Thames)? Clearly it could not.

Although the initial consortium was replaced by Olympia & York Canary Wharf Ltd (owned by the Reichmann brothers of Toronto, who have also developed the World Financial Centre in the Battery Park area of New York City), the scale of the development was not reduced significantly. As noted already, however, though tenants occupied the first phase from summer 1991, including some of the now familiar central tower, further phases are in doubt, given the project's financial crisis in 1992. While construction proceeded, the DLR was upgraded. Station platforms were lengthened to cope with double-length trains; headways between trains were shortened, and the system is now poised to cope with 12,000 passengers an hour on the link between Bank station and the Isle of Dogs.

An extension to Bank station shows symbolism at work again. The DLR was a vital part of the weaponry to market Docklands as an overspill area for the congested and expensive office floorspace of the City of London. Unfortunately, the overspill argument lost force after the property slump which started in 1989, and which resulted in almost 20 per cent of office floorspace in central London standing vacant in 1992 (chapter 2). The DLR's original overground terminus at Tower Gateway, alongside the Fenchurch Street to Southend railway, is reminiscent of those temporary termini

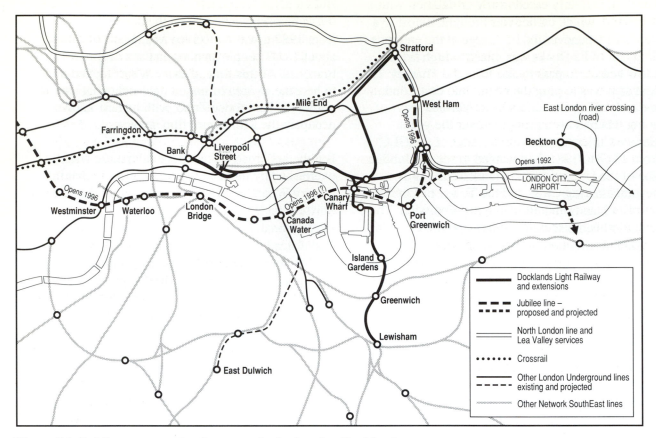

Figure 7.1 Public transport developments in the London Docklands.

built while the Victorian mainline railways pushed towards their grander stations around the rim of the central area. On the other hand the Bank terminus opened in 1991 is properly perceived as being at the very heart of the City of London, and is a significant interchange for users of the Underground system. The Bank to Canary Wharf journey takes only ten minutes.

Work is already well advanced on the 11-station extension of the DLR eastwards to Beckton (fig. 7.1), and with the necessary parliamentary approval, it is hoped that the DLR could be running southwards from Island Gardens to Greenwich and Lewisham by 1995. What has happened with rail provision is that the new and expanded networks have been development-led. Canary Wharf has been the prime cause of the upgrading of the DLR, and should be a financial partner in the latest Underground line, the extension of the Jubilee line from Green Park via Westminster and the Waterloo and London Bridge termini to Stratford via Canada Water (Surrey Docks), Canary Wharf and Port Greenwich (the Greenwich peninsula). This more than anything would properly integrate Docklands into the public

transport map in London, though the financial crisis of the Canary Wharf development in 1992 placed both Olympia & York's contribution and the scheme as a whole in some doubt.

In fact, what is now rapidly emerging is a redrawn map of accessibility in London in which the east side and the lower Thames corridor are no longer disadvantaged compared with the west. Stratford, now selected as a major channel tunnel rail interchange on the high speed link to King's Cross will also become a major interchange for Underground (Central, DLR and Jubilee lines) and rail (Liverpool Street and Crossrail services) passengers, and will offer easy access to the Isle of Dogs. This pattern of strategic planning *emerging* as if by accident is now familiar in Britain, and contrasts strongly with several other major cities. In Paris, for example, the even larger office development at La Défense (on the axis westwards from the Champs Elysées/Arc de Triomphe) followed the siting of the new RER (regional express) line there in 1970, all in accordance with carefully defined regional structure and investment strategies.

London City Airport: a catalyst for the regeneration of the Royals?

The Isle of Dogs has been put on the map by the DLR and the Enterprise Zone, and the Canary Wharf tower has punctuated London's skyline for all to see. The Royal Docks remain more intractable as a redevelopment challenge. For a start they are further downstream, poorly connected to the City and West End, and their very scale – four kilometres of water and dock walls from west to east – is forbidding. An audacious team of John Mowlem & Co as owner and operator, together with Brymon Airways and the LDDC, brought into existence what at first appeared a hair-brained proposal. Warehouses on the narrow finger of land between the Royal Albert and King George V Docks were demolished and replaced by the runway of the London City Airport, which opened in 1987. Short Take-Off and Landing aircraft (hence the earlier name of STOLport), principally the Canadian DeHavilland Dash-7 turbo-propellor model, offer a steeper than usual ascent on their hops to Brussels, Paris, Rotterdam and Strasbourg.

Approval was sought and examined at a public inquiry for aircraft such as the BAe 146 'whisper jet' to use London City Airport, and permission was granted in October 1991. As a consequence, all of the European capitals inside the arc from Lisbon, Rome, Budapest, Warsaw and Stockholm are now within reach of London City Airport (fig.

7.2). The title, London *City* Airport, is significant, its principal target being business people originating within or visiting the City of London and the adjacent West End just ten kilometres away. Local groups had expressed concern about the proximity of housing and a local school to the runway. But although groups like the Docklands Consultative Committee and the authors of the 'People's Plan' for Newham deplore the way in which the airport has sterilised the dock isthmus, they cannot dispute the way in which it has put Docklands in business travellers' magazines across Europe.

Road improvements

Access difficulties to and from Docklands have not been confined to public transport. The road network has long been incapable of accommodating the traffic demands of the area, not least traffic wishing to cross the River Thames downstream from the Tower of London. The two tunnels in Docklands – the Rotherhithe dating from the turn of the century, and the Blackwall with one bore of similar vintage and a second opened in the 1960s – have long aggravated queuing motorists, and the Rotherhithe has not been able to accommodate long and heavy vehicles around its tight under-the-river bends. In fact the link between London's North and South Circular roads is not a bridge or tunnel, but the Woolwich Ferry.

As with rail networks, the aim of road planning in Docklands has been to improve the area's connections with the rest of London and the strategic road network of the lower Thames and south-east England, and to improve accessibility within Docklands. Two agencies are responsible: the Department of Transport and the LDDC (see their joint publication dated 1991). LDDC road schemes have been funded out of the government grant to the corporation, whose income has of late been augmented by the corporation's receipts from land sales. Department of Transport (DTp) schemes are part of the nationally funded road programme, and have to compete with all other parts of the country clamouring for new roads and bypasses.

The LDDC's schemes are predominantly on the north bank, and when completed by 1993 will improve significantly east–west movements between the City of London onto and within the Isle of Dogs (including around Canary Wharf), and

Figure 7.2 **The flying range of services by jet from London City Airport as approved in October 1991.**

from the Island across the River Lea to and within the Royals. Most schemes (fig. 7.3) comprise four- or six-lane dual carriageway roads. Construction costs are abnormally high because the area is fractured by the River Lea and dock basins. The principal obstruction is Limehouse basin, which the Limehouse Link road has to tunnel beneath on its way to the Isle of Dogs. This is Britain's most costly road to date in cost per kilometre – a cost only tolerable as the price to be paid for securing an acceptable balance between accessibility and capacity on the one hand, and minimising longer-term environmental impact on the other. The shorter-term disturbance to residents during the construction phase attracted considerable publicity in 1991.

There are three main thrusts to the DTp programme. The first is the long-awaited East London River Crossing (ELRIC), a £300 million ten-kilometre scheme to link the North Circular Road at Beckton with the A2/M2 in south-east

London and north Kent. It has been subject to several delays, most recently because of a further public inquiry to examine the design of the high bridge across the Thames in view of the related issue of increasing the size of aircraft using London City Airport. Objectors at the inquiry have also been anxious to preserve an ancient and hitherto undisturbed area of woodland to the south of the river.

The Secretary of State for Transport approved the road, together with a widened and lowered bridge, in October 1991. Simultaneously, the European Commission questioned whether, despite the exhaustive inquiry process, Britain had formally satisfied the European Community directive on environmental impact assessment in the case of ELRIC and three other schemes. Assuming completion by the mid to late 1990s, the crossing will open up the Royals, especially to commuter traffic from north Kent, and in symbolic terms greatly improve the perceived accessibility of

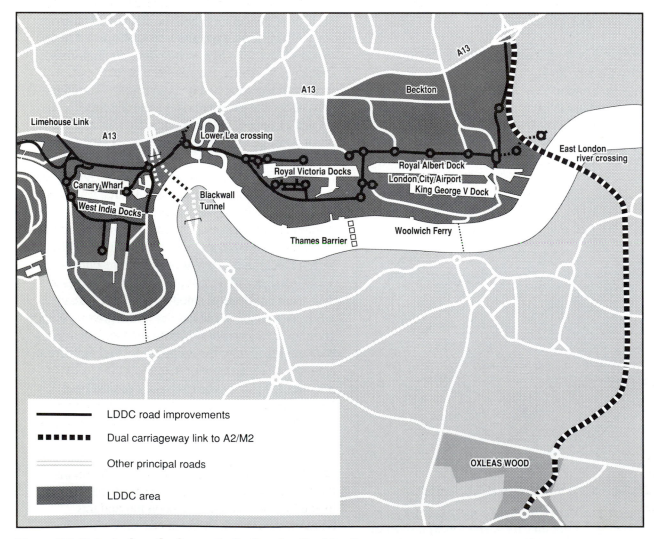

Figure 7.3 Principal road schemes in the London Docklands.

Docklands to the channel tunnel terminal near Folkestone.

The second DTp scheme is for a co-ordinated suite of improvements to significant bottlenecks along the A13 trunk road between Limehouse and Beckton. Apart from the altogether familiar tide of commuters' vehicles, the A13 also carries London's greatest load of heavy goods vehicles, many of which are destined for the Port of London Authority's Tilbury Docks (London's principal dock lies beyond London's boundary in Essex). There are seven junction improvements in all, which will aid flow along the artery and ease Docklands ingress and egress. The third DTp scheme, least advanced, is the proposal to construct a spur from the heavily congested Blackwall Tunnel to the Isle of Dogs, and by the late 1990s to construct a third bore for northbound tunnel traffic.

Taken together, these LDDC and DTp road schemes offer the prospect of a higher capacity of strategic and local roads within Docklands by the mid 1990s than anywhere else in London. It just so happens that in the interim the area appears to the driver or passenger as an uninterrupted traffic jam, whether caused by construction diversions or the totally inadequate inherited network. Favoured indeed are those fortunate enough to use the River Bus – 62-seater catamarans sailing to a 20-minute schedule between Charing Cross Pier and London City Airport, and offering a relaxed 35-minute journey between the airport and the City of London. Congestion apart, bus travellers have also benefited during the 1980s with the advent of new bus routes within and across the Docklands area.

Who funds the system improvements?

There are some fine examples of breathtaking civil engineering within Docklands, not least associated with the Limehouse Link tunnel and the Lower Lea crossing. But another significant kind of innovation must not be overlooked. In respect of both Underground railway, and road improvements, the government and local boroughs have sought to recoup part of the costs from developers. The principle was first developed for the Docklands Light Railway extension to Bank, £68 million out of a total of £400 million being paid by Olympia & York, the Canary Wharf developers. In the case of roads, the Limehouse Link, which will greatly improve access to the

Island, has provided a bounty for the local borough (Tower Hamlets), who, in an 'accord' with Olympia & York, are using a grant of £2 million from the developer to fund a variety of socially orientated projects. As noted above, Olympia & York were also due to contribute towards the estimated cost of the £1 billion Jubilee Line extension to Docklands and Stratford. However, by mid 1992, the financial uncertainty surrounding the Canary Wharf project called sharply into question both this specific contribution and also the wisdom of trying to fund public transport in this way.

An emerging vision of lower Thamesside

Malcolm Rifkind, the then Secretary of State for Transport, instructed British Rail in October 1991 to bring the channel tunnel rail link to London via Rainham and Stratford on the north bank of the Thames rather than on BR's preferred alignment through south-east London (fig. 7.4). In doing so he gave credence to the emerging concept of a 'lower Thames corridor' supported by his cabinet colleague Michael Heseltine (then Environment Secretary) and advocated by Peter Hall as special adviser to Mr Heseltine. Students of *realpolitik* will say that the easterly alignment was chosen to dissipate voters' hostility in marginal parliamentary constituencies in south-east London. The government spoke of reducing environmental damage and developing opportunities for economic growth.

The growth potential of the east Thames corridor was outlined seven years earlier in the annual review of regional strategy undertaken by the south-east regional planning conference (SERPLAN). Consultants appointed in 1989 examined private sector attitudes to the corridor. The rail announcement now gives the concept substance. The lower Thames, Docklands included, is now seen as London's gateway to mainland Europe. It becomes one end of a long 'channel funnel' rather than the London terminus of the channel tunnel rail link. Thus the Thames resumes its role as an artery linking London with the rest of the world, after a decade or more of being seen as little more than a physical barrier between north and south banks since the closure of the upstream docks. At an even larger scale, the decision enhances a view of London's eastern approaches as the link between the tunnel itself and the Midlands and north of England.

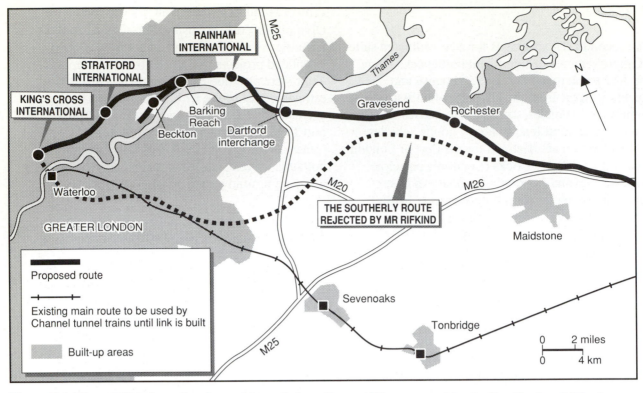

Figure 7.4 The rail link from the channel tunnel along the east Thames corridor to Stratford and King's Cross preferred by government in October 1991.

Photo: LDDC

London City Airport in the Royal Docks. The density of adjacent housing is clearly evident.

Following on from some of the ideas explored in chapter 3, it will be appreciated that the announcement of a consultants' study of the east Thames corridor as a kind of dispersed linear city raises questions about how the London boroughs and Essex and Kent counties and districts will relate to central government in any such regional growth scheme. Will the LDDC itself have ambitions of transubstantiation on the completion of its upstream mission, and view the Royals as a new base from which to fan out down the banks of the Thames and reduce east–west imbalances in the London region on an even grander scale?

Co-ordination

In any major schemes, such as those described in this chapter, design and construction is in many ways less problematic than the institutional organisation of the projects, and more especially, winning the initial commitment from central and local government, the LDDC, local occupiers and residents, and developers. Although there has been much criticism about seeming prevarication in the mid 1980s, and in the early 1990s a project such as the Jubilee Line extension is still far from certain, even sceptics will have to admit that transport in Docklands is now coming together. In a sense the

Passengers boarding the Docklands Light Railway. Photo: LDDC

sum of parts grows into a strategy – the reverse of devising a clear transport strategy a decade or so ago and driving through a related sequence of projects. But I suggest that the outcome from both approaches would have been broadly similar. Cynics might say that the lack of a formal transport plan means that there are no charges of failure to be pinned on the government or LDDC in their role as 'the planners'. On the other hand, the energetic enthusiasms of the initial team of LDDC board and officers shaping the area are evident in the Docklands Light Railway and the London City Airport. More recently, ministers in the Department of Transport have made the case for Docklands within the Treasury and with developers, and have undoubtedly helped to give coherence and the necessary guarantees of government commitment.

8 The great Docklands housing boom

Darrel Crilley

Introduction

Few issues in the redevelopment of Docklands have been as contentious as that of the availability and affordability of housing. Whilst private housing for sale has been produced in dramatic quantities (table 8.1) in a wide array of styles and sold at prices which have risen to match those of higher-status areas of London, the housing needs of residents in areas within and surrounding the official Docklands territory have gone unmet and, until recently, largely unheeded. The London Docklands Household Survey (LDDC, 1991b) certainly confirms the shift in tenure over the last decade: a rise in the proportion of owner-occupiers from 5 per cent to 36 per cent and a decline in local authority tenure from 83 per cent to 44 per cent (fig. 8.1). Moreover, as LDDC acknowledged in 1991, approximately 1500 new housing units stand empty: a testimony to the rampant speculation in the Docklands land market. Yet despite the Docklands housing boom, the indications are that the plight of many residents has actually worsened: the number of families officially accepted as homeless in the five Docklands boroughs (including Greenwich and Lewisham) rose by 284 per cent between 1981 and 1988, leaving boroughs such as Tower Hamlets with the number of people in temporary accommodation well above the London average. All boroughs report that extensive funds are required to refurbish their existing stock and create new dwellings; the three

boroughs also have nearly twice as many overcrowded households as is typical in London; and, as a final measure of the difficulties, the total number of dwellings considered unfit for habitation was very high (table 8.2). Meanwhile, amidst this deepening housing crisis stand many expensive new housing units for sale, in part newly built and in part conversions of old warehouses, and partly either unsold or unoccupied.

In areas of Docklands such as Wapping we can see two opposing tendencies taking shape side by side in the provision of housing. On the one hand is a process of gentrification involving plush conversions of historic warehouses, refurbishment of former council blocks to make attractive apartments for new professionals and a growing number of houses designed by prestigious architects. Many of these are private and exclusive developments, protected by elaborate security systems, serviced by lavish leisure facilities and usually enjoying the views and scenery of the Thames for which higher prices can be demanded. Indeed, with occasional exceptions such as the hard-fought scheme for Cherry Garden Pier housing on the Bermondsey riverbank, the whole of the waterfront has been taken over by luxurious private schemes. On the other hand, we witness a process of deterioration and decay of council housing stock, frequently occurring just across the street, brought about by a cumulative lack of funds for its upkeep. The question which must be

Table 8.1   Housing activity within the LDDC area (cumulative totals)

Date	Units started			Units completed		
	LDDC land	Non-LDDC land	Total	LDDC land	Non-LDDC land	Total
1981/82	601	–	–	–	–	–
1982/83	1624	–	–	339	–	–
1983/84	3073	885	3958	1148	349	1497
1984/85	4702	2266	6968	1810	588	2398
1985/86	5972	3430	9402	3103	1127	4230
1986/87	7370	4605	11975	4210	2718	6928
1987/88	8567	6458	15025	5602	3180	8782

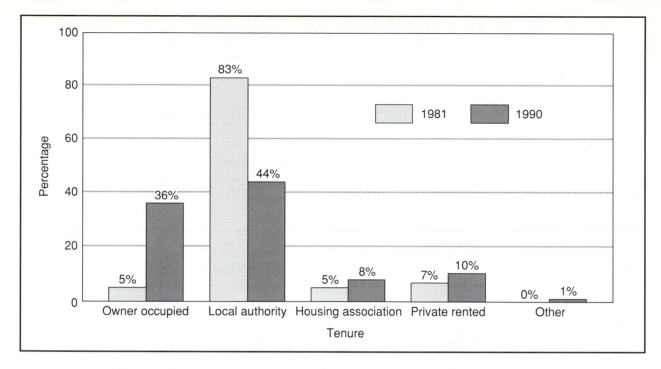

Figure 8.1 **Percentage distribution of households by tenure: 1981 compared to 1990.**
Source: London Docklands Household Survey (1991b), p. 46

answered is how, at a time of such mounting need, could the unique land resources offered by Docklands be used to subsidise what is almost exclusively private development? How were local people excluded from enjoying the benefits of London's greatest housing boom since the construction of high-rise towers in the 1960s? An answer is found in the intersection of four factors: the initial housing 'policy' adopted by the LDDC; the mechanisms of housing provision; the destruction of local authority housing programmes; and the mismatch between the housing funds local people possess relative to the cost of access to the new housing.

The LDDC's early housing policy

At the time of its inception, the administrative area of the LDDC was dominated by public sector housing (more than 80 per cent) to an extent that was deemed 'unhealthy', 'unbalanced' and inimical to the spirit of 'regeneration'. Accordingly, one of the LDDC's central objectives has been to reverse this, promoting the construction of housing for owner occupation as the spearhead of redevelopment: if young, affluent residents could be attracted to live in the area and private house builders enticed to take up land, then the future regeneration would look brighter. The

Table 8.2   **Unfit[1] dwellings, April 1988**

Borough	Public sector	% of stock	Private sector	% of stock	Total	% of stock
Newham	21,777	63	25,200	50	46,977	56
Southwark	24,006	34	13,355	48	37,361	38
Tower Hamlets	23,757	44	3,155	25	31,416	46

Source: LDDC (1989)

[1] Total dwellings which were unfit, or lacked one or more basic amenities, or were in need of substantial renovation to a cost exceeding £6,500

Table 8.3   Housing starts in the LDDC area by tenure as at 31 March 1988

Area	For sale	Shared ownership	For rent	Total
Royal Docks	2776	229	945	3950
Surrey Docks	4271	142	588	5001
Isle of Dogs	2819	22	60	2901
Wapping	2818	133	222	3173
Total	12,684	526	1815	15,025

Source: LDDC (1989)

role of housing was clearly symbolic: it would change jaundiced perceptions of the area by transforming industrial dereliction into a scene for the 'ultimate urban lifestyle', to adopt one of the developer's favourite clichés. In pursuit of this goal, the LDDC did not act as a housing authority with a direct responsibility to build houses, but operated as a land broker, assembling, reclaiming, servicing and marketing plots of land to private house builders. Hence, whereas local authorities viewed the vacant land of Docklands as a one-off opportunity to provide substantial housing for rent, the LDDC interpreted its goal as the encouragement of a range of housing options to promote a 'balanced' and 'integrated' community.

On the land vested in it, the LDDC was, however, committed to two things. Firstly, maintaining a balance between 50 per cent of housing for sale, 25 per cent for rent and a further 25 per cent to be available through shared ownership schemes. Secondly, since 1983 it had a low-cost home ownership policy whereby a developer was obliged to produce a specified proportion of dwellings built on land acquired from the LDDC for sale below a fixed, 'affordable' price (since 1986, £40,000) and on which 'local' residents were given first preference. One of the most persistent criticisms levelled at the LDDC is that neither of these obligations has been honoured. In relation to the first stipulation, on LDDC-owned land, over 80 per cent of dwellings started had been for owner occupation, with minimal amounts of rented housing (table 8.3). Similarly, aside from the difficulties of deciding an appropriate level of affordability, by 1989 the LDDC was compelled to admit in its Housing Strategy Review that a combination of rampant speculation and no improvements in local ability to buy had nullified the affordability strategy. By 1986, just three years

after the strategy was announced, rapid inflation in the Docklands housing market had ensured that less than 10 per cent of housing was for sale at or under £40,000. Quoting a study by the East London Housing Authority, they belatedly acknowledged a list of factors that had long been the clarion call of opposition organisations such as the Docklands Forum. These were chiefly: not one household in the survey was in a position to afford the mortgage to purchase a so-called 'affordable' dwelling; that the gulf between ability to pay and market prices in Docklands was so great that not one household could afford to take out a 50 per cent equity stake on a new Docklands home; and that where units did appear affordable (now considered in the region of £70,000) they were inappropriate as family housing (the majority were one-bedroom flats) and confined to certain areas of Docklands (such as Beckton). By 1990, numerous surveys of new residents in the Docklands had shown the limited chance it afforded to council tenants in the surrounding boroughs. New developments, contrary to the claims of the LDDC, are overwhelmingly not occupied by former tenants of the local council (see also chapter 10). 'Affordability' has turned out to be little more than a hollow promise and an overture aimed to provide an appearance of doing something to address local needs.

The method of housing provision

Criticism of the LDDC has also centred on its subsidy of private profit at the expense of public need by selling public land off to developers at discount prices and encouraging a boom in land and housing markets that prices local authorities and residents out of the market. On the first issue, an internal audit report from the LDDC in 1987 revealed a lack of consistency in their disposal of public land and acknowledged that the public may be short-changed in the release of land to developers. In Wapping, for instance, Regalian Properties paid £4.63 million per acre for a site called Hermitage Basin, yet for Silver Walk in Rotherhithe, it paid just £1.03 million per acre, a figure considered to be well below its potential asking price.

As the examples in table 8.4 show, house prices in Docklands rocketed prior to the end of 1987 – often doubling in less than a year – allowing speculators to buy flats at low prices, hold them unoccupied, and then put them back on the market at higher rates. Often properties were being sold and resold 'off the drawing board', that is prior to construction being completed. Though this market has now dried up, it allowed a multitude of individuals to amass large personal gains quickly by speculating that their properties would continue to rise in price. Frequently developers were encouraging this; Kentish Homes for instance guaranteeing a 16.5 per cent increase in value in 18 months after the completion of their developments. The main consequences were twofold: house prices were pushed up to levels well beyond the buying capacity of local residents and the LDDC benefited from the knock-on effect this had in raising land values, a major source of the LDDC's finance.

The decimation of local authority housing programmes

Focusing on the LDDC tells only half the story. We must also ask what opportunities have been lost. On this score, it is clear that the plans of local authorities to meet the housing needs of their residents have been thwarted by the loss of essential land resources to the LDDC coupled with a lack of requisite finance to provide public sector housing. Throughout the 1980s local boroughs protested at the vesting of land in the LDDC that had been targeted for the provision of low-rent housing: they now no longer had the essential land resources even if they had the money to build. Tower Hamlets, for example, owned 216 hectares of house-building land prior to the imposition of the LDDC, but soon had this reduced to 3.5 hectares. Southwark's land bank was similarly depleted. The substantial site of the Surrey Docks which the council had purchased in the 1970s and on which housing provision had already begun in 1981 was largely appropriated for the LDDC's purposes leaving Southwark with just six hectares for council housing. Ironically, however, as the 1980s drew to a close and many new luxury developments remained substantially unsold, local authorities regained some housing through taking out leases on private developments or being given 'replacement' housing to compensate for

Table 8.4   Examples of the house price boom in Docklands in the mid-1980s

1. Isle of Dogs (Clippers' Quay) 2-bedroom flat

Date	£
June 1985	47,500
January 1986	74,950
June 1986	125,000
March 1987	199,950

2. Surrey Docks (Brunswick Quay, Greenland Dock)

Date	1-bedroom flat (£)	3-bedroom house (£)
January 1985	29,995	53,500
June 1986	60,000	95,000
September 1987	68,000	110,000
January 1989	75,000	140,000

3. Wapping

Date	1-bedroom flat, Gun wharf (£)	Date	2-bedroom house, South Quay (£)
July 1984	73,000	January 1985	37,850
February 1986	115,000	September 1986	90,000
March 1987	185,000	May 1987	105,000
March 1988	215,000		

Sources: (1) DCC (1988); (2) Southwark Borough Planning Department (nd); (3) Coupland (1989)

demolition of estates to make way for infrastructural developments. Thus, Tower Hamlets council has leased parts of Cascades on the Isle of Dogs and Thomas More Court in Wapping to homeless families, and both Roy Square, Narrow Street, Limehouse and Timber Wharves on the Isle of Dogs are to be occupied by council tenants displaced to make way for the new Limehouse Link road. Such gains remain piecemeal and minor, however, in relation to the size of the problem. From a cynical perspective, the purchase of Timber Wharves is seen as one more instance of subsidising private development since the developer – Ideal Homes – had managed to dispose of just 37 out of 421 units on the open market. There is also concern that because management of the block will be the responsibility of the East London Housing Authority, rents will rise to unaffordable levels and residents will have no security of tenure. As Isle of Dogs councillor Terese Shanahan argues:

> If tenants are forced out by high rents in a couple of years, the property owner will regain possession ready for sale just when the housing market starts to take off again. If there are no guarantees that these properties will remain for council tenants, Timber Wharves will have returned to the private sector it never really left.

The key point remains, therefore, that the act of vesting the critical resource of land in the LDDC has, at least in Tower Hamlets, largely pre-empted the entire housing strategy that was sabotaged in 1980.

Just as handicapping have been drastic cuts in central allocations to local boroughs for housing investment (table 8.5) and continuing losses of existing stock under the 1980 Right to Buy legislation. Even though sales rates are exceptionally low in the Docklands boroughs, the loss of council housing units constitutes a once-and-for-all loss of a resource. Additionally, local authorities are now expected to generate capital to invest in housing from proceeds of council house sales, but in Tower Hamlets and Newham with their concentration of 'difficult-to-sell' tower blocks and sales rates which are amongst the lowest in the country, this yields but a trickle of funds. Further to this, the initiative of authorities is frustrated by rigid controls over how they can utilise what funds are available: increasingly, they are being compelled to channel funds into the renovation of what already exists and leave expansion of social housing to Housing Associations.

Local ability to purchase

The notion that local residents would be able to participate in the private housing market itself was at best idealistic, at worst cynical and misguided. The uncertain economic position of sizeable segments of the local population, characterised by high unemployment rates, underemployment, work in informal activities and the threat of continuing loss of manufacturing industry, means that they have neither the stocks of economic wealth to raise the initial deposits on houses nor sufficient income flows to meet mortgage repayments. The Docklands Housing Needs Survey, carried out in 1987 by the London Research Centre, makes this point forcefully. At that date, some 75 per cent of households in the three boroughs had annual incomes of under £8500, £3500 short of the minimum sum required to raise the mortgage on an 'affordable' property. For ethnic minority households the position is acknowledged to be even more precarious: home ownership is a remote possibility.

Hope for the future?

During 1989–90 there were substantial improvements in Docklands housing. On the one hand, private residential developers who

Table 8.5 Department of the Environment housing investment programme, allocations 1988–90

Borough	1988/89 (£ million)	1989/90 (£ million)	Real change (%)
Newham	18.1	14.7	–23
Southwark	29.2	22.7	–27
Tower Hamlets	15.5	12.3	–25

Source: LDDC (1989)

Distinctive housing by the Thames on the Isle of Dogs.   Photo: LDDC

New housing in Wapping with council-sector tower blocks in the background.   Photo: Philip Ogden

specialised in Docklands property became bankrupt and went into receivership, their schemes often being acquired by local authorities and housing associations. On the other hand, the LDDC rethought its housing strategy and by 1991 there were tentative steps towards implementation. Three major schemes were approved and allotted direct financial backing by the LDDC as a

Photo: Philip Ogden

Warehouses converted or about to be converted for residential use.

supplement to funds from the central government Housing Corporation. The main initiatives were the Winsor Estate in Beckton where 409 rented homes were to be provided at rents which approximate to 'fair' rents (i.e. based on ability to pay) and 70 per cent of which would be reserved for people on Newham council's waiting lists; 175 homes for rent at Masthouse Terrace on the Isle of Dogs; and the biggest gain of all to come from the refurbishment of a former council estate in the Surrey Docks, named 'Downtown'. This now yields 639 units for rent, 148 shared ownership, 18 for sale at 'affordable' prices and 161 for sale at market prices. Added to this, the LDDC has increased its contribution to refurbishment of existing estates from a mere £2.75 million pounds between 1981 and 1987 to £6.83 million in 1988/89. The nature of the refurbishment it funds has also changed for the better. It had been a point of contention that LDDC funds were used for cosmetic purposes of external environmental improvements to make the area slightly more agreeable for new residents. The LDDC is now moving away from such tactics as tree planting and adding flowerbeds, new windows and Grecian pillars to entrance ways, towards internal refitting of local authority blocks. Though these are the most substantial gains to date and, had they been initiated in the early 1980s, could have ameliorated the local housing crisis, it remains clear that, as the size of the borough's housing problem has escalated, this may be all too little too late. The Winsor Terrace initiative, to give one example, has to be considered in the context of 1556 Newham families accepted as homeless and 4345 families on the council's waiting list. Even now, there are grounds for caution and doubt: the LDDC is prohibited by government from making contributions to refurbishment of more than 25 per cent and is yet to honour current commitments; rent levels in the new schemes vary widely and are liable to rise significantly; there is an inadequate strategy for black and ethnic minority groups most in need; and the LDDC's allocation for housing provision has decreased, not increased, between 1989 and 1992.

9 Employment

Andrew Church

The Docklands economy in 1981

Employment levels in Docklands and the surrounding East London area had fallen sharply in the 1970s. In the five East London boroughs (Tower Hamlets, Southwark, Newham, Greenwich and Lewisham) the number of jobs fell by 16 per cent between 1971 and 1981 – from 601,400 to 506,000. The manufacturing sector was particularly hard hit, losing 44 per cent of total jobs, and employment in transport and communication also fell by 40 per cent. The situation in the smaller LDDC area was even worse. In just three years between 1978 and 1981 10,000 jobs were lost, a decline of 27 per cent.

Despite this decline, the Docklands economy in 1981 still contained a high proportion of manufacturing jobs – 41 per cent of jobs in the LDDC area compared to 19 per cent in Greater London. This reflected the fact that East London had been one of the key areas for manufacturing in London.

Not surprisingly, decline had been accompanied by high unemployment. In the three Docklands boroughs of Tower Hamlets, Newham and Southwark, the unemployment rate was 15 per cent in April 1981 and had risen sharply by January 1982 to 18 per cent. Again, the outlook in the LDDC area was even bleaker and unemployment rose from 22 per cent to 26 per cent in the same period, so that one in four people were out of work.

The aims of the LDDC

Regeneration policies in the 1970s under the Docklands Joint Committee had emphasised the need to retain and expand existing employment, and also to attract new investment especially in manufacturing and transport companies which would require workers with skills typical of local residents. Success was limited: 1.35 million square feet of factory space was built between 1976 and 1980; major investments included Billingsgate fishmarket; in Wapping construction work started on the News International printworks and the World Trade Centre was expanded. However,

whilst 800 jobs came to Docklands, 8000 were lost as part of the general decline in East London. Much of the new industrial space stayed empty.

The LDDC ushered in a very different approach to employment creation. Stimulating the property market was seen as the route to economic regeneration. LDDC expenditure on land, infrastructure and marketing, combined with the incentive of the Enterprise Zone, was designed to encourage property investors to construct new commercial and industrial units. These new buildings would then be occupied by job-creating businesses. Employment creation was thus closely linked to the response of the property market.

The LDDC was keen to attract certain types of employment. The 1970s emphasis on manufacturing and transport was gone. The LDDC claimed that 'sunrise' industries were needed in Docklands since they would provide secure long-term employment opportunities into the next century. In 1983, the LDDC defined the growth sectors it was hoping to attract: firms in telecommunications and information technology; financial services and other City of London activities; printing and media activities; bio-technology; leisure and tourism.

The LDDC was also intended to stem decline and assist existing firms. It offers business advice to both new and existing firms and is able to provide loans and rent relief grants. In 1988/89 the LDDC spent £750,000 on industry support (0.6 per cent of total grant received), but this had fallen to £221,000 in 1990/91. These low figures suggest that the LDDC was more concerned with new growth sectors rather than maintaining the existing firms.

The nature of employment change since 1981

Total employment in Docklands hardly changed between 1981 and 1985, rising from 27,213 to 28,180. This reflected the slow start to the area's redevelopment. By 1987, the figure had risen to 36,385 with a further increase to 53,000 by 1991

Table 9.1   The nature of employment attracted to the LDDC area 1981–90

1980 Standard industrial classification	Employment attracted 1981–90 Number	%
Agriculture, forestry, fishing	54	0.1
Energy/water	233	0.6
Manufacture: minerals/chemicals	237	0.6
Metal goods / vehicles	798	1.9
Other manufacturing	7968	19.3
Construction	5805	14.0
Distribution, hotels/catering	6076	14.7
Transport/communication	2959	7.1
Banking, finance, insurance etc	9824	23.7
Other services	4594	11.1
Not properly classified	2873	6.9
Total employment attracted	41421	100.0

Source: Association of London Authorities and Docklands Consultative Committee (1991)

(LDDC, 1991a). In addition, in 1987 and 1990 there were between 5000 and 6000 temporary construction jobs in Docklands.

Table 9.1 indicates the types of employment attracted to Docklands between 1981 and 1990 and includes both new employment and employment transferred from elsewhere. Jobs available increased by 41,421 and this employment growth in Docklands was concentrated in three sectors: 'other manufacturing'; distribution, hotel and catering; banking finance, insurance and leasing. These sectors accounted for 57.8 per cent of the jobs attracted to Docklands. The growth in 'other manufacturing' was mainly the result of the relocation of five major national print works from Fleet Street – the *Guardian*, *The Daily/Sunday Telegraph*, Associated Newspapers (*Daily/Sunday Mail*), News International (*Sun*, *The Times*, *The Sunday Times*, *News of the World*, *Today*) and *The Financial Times*. They have also been joined by the offices of the press agency Reuters.

The importance of large firms relocating is also apparent in the banking, finance, insurance and leasing sector. Sixty per cent of growth in this sector between 1981 and 1987 was accounted for by seven large firms moving to Docklands from the City of London.

The influx of jobs in distribution, hotels and catering initially stemmed from the opening of new retail distribution units, such as the Asda superstores at the Isle of Dogs and Beckton, the Surrey Quays shopping centre, where over 1000

people work, and DIY and other retail warehouses on sites in Beckton that were formerly part of the London Industrial Park, now, as a sign of the Docklands economy in the 1980s, renamed the London Retail Park. This sector will grow in future as demand from business and tourists stimulates the hotel trade in Docklands. One 390-bedroom hotel has already opened in the Surrey Quays. Page (1989) estimates that if all the hotels proposed in Docklands are constructed they would provide approximately 5000 beds employing between 7000 and 9500 people. Women form a high proportion of workers in these sectors.

These sectoral changes mean that the economy of Docklands is now dominated by the service industry. This pattern is likely to continue into the future. Predictions of future job growth vary enormously. Canary Wharf when completed was to contain approximately 50–60,000 workers. Optimists at the LDDC suggested there would be a total of 200,000 jobs in Docklands by the end of the century, but a more pessimistic view from the Docklands Forum community group predicted 116,000–120,000 by 1998. The recent slowdown in the property market and the financial crisis of the Canary Wharf scheme have, however, made serious estimates of employment growth extremely difficult.

The nature of employment change
There has been considerable argument over the effectiveness of the LDDC's property-based approach to job creation. The total employment levels disguise the details of change. Many of the

jobs that have come to Docklands since 1981 are in firms moving from elsewhere in London and bringing their workforces with them. At the same time many jobs are being lost in Docklands. The jobs balance sheet for 1981–90 is shown in table 9.2.

Between 1981 and 1990 there was an inflow of 41,421 jobs to Docklands of which 60 per cent were transfers from elsewhere. Opponents of the LDDC use these figures to argue that since the number of new, as opposed to transfer, jobs is 3,973 less than the number of jobs lost then the LDDC has yet to achieve a net increase in employment. Furthermore, the large outflow is seen as an indication of the LDDC's failure to safeguard existing jobs.

LDDC supporters would respond by claiming that the outflow is not something the LDDC could or should try to prevent. Jobs being shed by firms in Docklands or job losses due to firms relocating out of Docklands are viewed as the unavoidable outcome of market forces as firms restructure their operations to maintain profitability. In addition, it is hoped that the future will provide plenty of new job opportunities due to labour turnover in transferred jobs creating new vacancies. Nevertheless, many LDDC opponents, whose concern is the locally unemployed, feel that future promises do not compensate for job losses in the 1980s.

The causes of employment change
The political debates over the LDDC's impact in terms of job creation are important, but it is also

Table 9.2   The dynamics of employment change in London Docklands, 1981–90

Total employment 1981	27,213
Gross employment increase 1981–90	+ 41,421
Gross employment decrease 1981–90	– 20,532
Net change 1981–90	+ 20,889
Total employment 1990	48,102
Gross employment increase comprised:	
Jobs transferred from elsewhere:	24,862
New jobs not previously located elsewhere:	16,559
Gross employment increase 1981–90	+ 41,421

Source: Association of London Authorities (1991)

necessary to identify why the economy of Docklands has changed in the 1980s. Some of the LDDC's target growth sectors have not materialised. Apart from some telecommunication installations that employ very few people, 'hi-tech' activities in information and bio-technology have not become part of the Docklands economy as the LDDC hoped. So why have certain industries grown in Docklands?

There is plenty of evidence to show that LDDC policies and incentives have attracted firms to Docklands. One survey of 241 firms who had moved to the Isle of Dogs since 1981 found that for 19 per cent, financial incentives were their main reason for moving there, while another 18 per cent cited the availability of premises (London Borough of Tower Hamlets, 1988). Whilst these local policy factors are partly responsible for employment change, there is evidence that national and international processes have also been an important influence (chapter 2).

Many of the larger firms in the three key growth sectors have expanded in Docklands as part of a wider restructuring process in response to changes in technology and the competitive conditions of the national and global economy.

Financial services expanded rapidly in the nearby City of London in the mid 1980s. Rajan and Fryatt (1988) show that employment in the City's six major financial service industries grew from 157,000 in 1984 to 195,000 in 1987, a remarkable 25 per cent growth. The late 1970s and early 1980s had seen the growth of new forms of securitised debt, such as Euro-bonds. This process of securitisation was accompanied by companies diversifying their activities and operating on an increasingly international basis with the help of new technology, all of which stimulated growth. Expansion was given a further impetus by government deregulation in the Financial Services Act of 1986 known as the 'Big Bang'. This saw a massive influx of foreign capital into the City of London, leading to a series of mergers and take-overs.

The outcome of this expansion was an increased demand for office space. Rents in Docklands were at least half those in the City of London and this attracted some firms to the area. However, employment growth in the City was largely over by 1987. Since then, companies have been rationalising their operations, creating a well-publicised spate of City redundancies which have increased during the recession. Ironically, Docklands has benefited to some extent from this process as firms looking to cut costs and improve productivity rationalise a number of offices at several locations into one base in Docklands. A good example was the accountancy firm Littlejohn Frazer, who amalgamated several offices in London into a purpose-built office block in the Enterprise Zone.

The same mix of local, national and international processes lies behind the expansion of printing and retail services. The large retail companies such as Tesco and Asda have opened branches in Docklands as part of their national competitive strategies as they expanded rapidly in the 1980s. Inner London locations provided an alternative to expensive out-of-town sites where planning permission was often harder to obtain.

In the national print industry, falling company profits in the late 1970s had increased pressure for rationalisation, especially the introduction of new technology that would dramatically reduce costs. Strong Fleet Street unions often opposed the changes in staffing levels and working conditions that would result. A geographical move was often the easiest way for firms to reorganise. New purpose-built premises would accommodate the new machinery and trade unions found it harder to oppose the changes occurring during a move. Indeed, News International simply sacked all their workers in Fleet Street and took on new employees in Wapping, resulting in a long and bitter industrial dispute.

Docklands has proved to be a convenient element in a wider restructuring process of these industries. This fact has been recognised by the LDDC, which has opportunistically harnessed the outcomes of restructuring to bring firms to Docklands.

The same analysis can be applied to employment loss. Local forces in the form of the LDDC are again important. Up to April 1989, the LDDC had relocated 142 firms out of Docklands. In a small number of cases the move harmed the firms' operations and jobs were lost. A number of other firms simply cashed in on the rising land values and left the area. Large numbers of jobs have been lost by multinational companies restructuring their plants in Docklands. For example, Tate and Lyle, the largest manufacturing employer in Docklands, shed 700 jobs between 1984 and 1987 in response to falling profits in cane sugar processing, due to a declining market and EC sugar cane import quotas.

Local employment and the training debate

Despite the inflow of jobs to Docklands the LDDC has received considerable criticism over the issue of employment for local residents. In the early 1980s, the LDDC was hoping that a 'trickle-down' process would allow local residents to fill job vacancies that appeared as a result of new jobs or labour turnover in transferred and existing firms.

But Docklands is part of the London labour market and there will be considerable in- and out-commuting. Figures on commuting patterns suggest that the effect of the 'trickle-down' process has been limited. One survey (RISUL, 1988) calculated that, of the 20,000 jobs transferred or created in Docklands between 1981 and 1987, 25 per cent had gone to residents of the Docklands boroughs (Tower Hamlets, Newham and Southwark). This is compared to another survey (London Borough of Tower Hamlets, 1988) which found that 60 per cent of jobs in firms on the Isle of Dogs established prior to 1981 were filled by residents of the surrounding borough of Tower Hamlets. The problem was that local residents were getting few of the new jobs and yet many were employed in older local firms that were shedding employment or closing down.

In the early 1980s, unemployment in Docklands rose sharply due to the national recession, a lack of labour demand in London generally, and the local availability of public housing which provides homes for those most likely to be unemployed and which in turn leads to concentrations of unemployment in inner London. The unemployment totals in the three Docklands boroughs rose from 36,000 in July 1981 when the LDDC was established, to a peak of over 55,000 in late 1985. By 1985 local unemployment rates ranged from 17.5 per cent in Newham to 21.8 per cent in Tower Hamlets, both way above a rate of 11.6 per cent for Greater London.

At the same time, political pressure was growing on the LDDC to develop policies that would allow local residents to gain more of the incoming jobs. In 1988, a House of Commons Committee with a majority of Conservative MPs concluded that 'the LDDC's approach to education, training and employment has been very limited, poorly monitored and not at all successful' (Employment Committee, 1988).

The LDDC had taken some action on training in the mid 1980s. An Information Technology

Training Centre (ITEC) had opened and the Skillnet initiative supported by the local councils was set up in 1985 to co-ordinate training provision and put on new courses where gaps in provision existed. However, the situation was still far from satisfactory. Local unemployment remained high and at the same time local employers were complaining of skill shortages. In addition, a number of training schemes had high drop-out rates as people left before completion.

Since 1988 the LDDC has increased expenditure on training. In six years, between 1981 and 1987, £4.6 million was spent on training, but in the next two years £2.8 million was spent, a far higher rate of expenditure. In 1989 the LDDC predicted it would spend £23 million by 1993 on 'job providing' initiatives, the majority of which would go on training and education; £10 million of this money went towards the recently opened Tower Hamlets Further Education College on a new site in Docklands. In addition, LDDC funding has provided extra childcare facilities to allow women with children to take advantage of new employment opportunities.

The LDDC now claims to provide support for 5000 training places. Providing support is a vague term since the LDDC contribution to a training place might be a quite small proportion of the total cost. However, this is a big increase on the 1500 places supported in 1988, but still less than the 7000 supported by the Merseyside Development Corporation in an area where needs are perhaps even greater.

The LDDC is not the only agency trying to make the links between regeneration and local residents. Accords, agreements and compacts have been signed between developers, employers, the LDDC and local authorities. The Canary Wharf Agreement between Olympia & York, the developers of Canary Wharf, and the Borough of Tower Hamlets meant that the developers were to provide £2.5 million for a training trust and to guarantee 2000 jobs for local residents, though the financial crisis at Olympia & York in 1992 threw cold water on these optimistic aims. Local Education Compacts also aim to create a stronger link between employers and school leavers.

It is still very hard to assess the overall effect of training in Docklands. For many local residents it may be too little too late. In the early 1980s the LDDC often argued that it had to wait for regeneration to get underway to ensure it provided the right type of training linked to new employers. This is true in terms of understanding employers' needs, but it is not a justification for not taking action earlier in relation to the needs of local residents. It had been clear throughout the 1970s that training and education needs in east London were very basic. Many people needed training in basic life skills, literacy and numeracy. They would require training to benefit from *any* type of regeneration.

Earlier action might have helped some local residents weather the recession. Instead, east London has been hit hard by the downturn in the national economy. Unemployment in the three Docklands boroughs in July 1991 was 47,570, which is higher than the figure of 36,000 when the LDDC was established in July 1981. This is in spite of numerous changes in the statistics that lower the official unemployment figures. Even in the smaller LDDC area this pattern is repeated. The figures are far less accurate but they suggest that in July 1981 3550 people were unemployed and this rose to a peak of 5000 in 1986. By March 1990 it had fallen to about 2700 only to rise again to over 4000 by July 1991. The national economic recovery in the mid and late 1980s plus a decade of inner-city policy have not solved the problem of high unemployment in Docklands and east London.

Conclusion

The message on employment in Docklands is fairly clear. A property-led approach will bring jobs to an area, the majority of these being transfers. In a complex metropolitan economy like London's, many of these jobs will go to people commuting into the area, but some local residents may gain employment. Nevertheless the 'trickle-down' effect will not work. The main beneficiaries of regeneration in employment terms are unlikely to be those most in need. Training and education must be key elements of any regeneration strategy and they must have a major role at the start.

Note
Unless stated otherwise all the factual information in this chapter has been extracted from the report 'Employment in Docklands' produced by the Docklands Forum and Andrew Church, Birkbeck College, University of London. This extensive 123-page report explores many of the issues raised in this chapter in far more detail and also lists the sources of factual information. This report can be obtained from the Docklands Forum, 192 Hanbury Street, London E1 4NS (price £10, ISBN 1 87245306 6)

10 Populations old and new

Ray Hall and Philip Ogden

Population, perhaps more than any other variable, illustrates the dramatic changes that have taken place in Docklands since 1981. In terms of London as a whole in the 1980s, the Docklands' wards were amongst the fastest growing in the capital and contributed to the reversal of inner London's population decline. There has thus been a remarkable turnaround in the population loss experienced by much of the area for nearly thirty years and indeed the population in the LDDC zone is projected to increase threefold from the 1981 figure of a little over 38,000 to 115,000 by 2001. The London Docklands Household Survey shows that already by 1990 the population of the LDDC area had increased to over 61,000: between 1981 and 1990 the population of the Wapping area had risen by 72 per cent, the Isle of Dogs by 26 per cent, the Royal Docks by 88 per cent and the Surrey Docks by 65 per cent. Moreover the demographic and social characteristics of new arrivals are in marked contrast to those of pre-1981 residents.

The key questions we wish to answer here are: How distinctive was the demographic structure of the population in the LDDC zone at the time of its creation in 1981? What are the population projections up to the end of the century? What are the characteristics of new residents moving into the area? The answers to these questions are of considerable importance in determining, for example, educational and health needs, as well as contributing to the general discussion about what sort of community is taking shape in Docklands.

How much do we know?

As mentioned elsewhere in this *Update*, the recency of change in Docklands means that much of the detail is inevitably unclear. However, the 1981 census was taken just before the creation of the LDDC, so that we do have a good portrait of the population characteristics of the area before major change took place. For population change during the 1980s, two sources are of value: the full household survey carried out by the LDDC in 1990 and the Census of Population in April 1991. The results of the latter were not available at the time of writing. We are able to piece together information from the population projections to the year 2000 from the London Research Centre; and from surveys carried out on behalf of the LDDC by estate agents and by other researchers.

In what follows, the geographical coverage varies: the LDDC area consists of all or part of eight wards (the basic unit for local elections, also used by the census) within the three boroughs (fig. 10.1). For details from the 1981 census, and change between 1981 and 1990, we are able to give information for the exact areas covered by the LDDC zone. For population change between 1971 and 1981 and for projections to 2000, we have to use information on the wards as a whole, including those sections outside the Docklands proper.

Population change 1971–81

The eight wards, of which some part falls within the area of the LDDC, had a population of 82,416 in 1971, which by 1981 had fallen by 16.6 per cent, only slightly below that of inner London as a whole with a decline of 17.6 per cent. The detailed geography of population decline shows that much of the area differed sharply from the inner London average (table 10.1). The western part of the area, the wards of St Katharine's and Shadwell, experienced declines of only 1.9 and 1.8 per cent respectively since people were already being attracted to the redeveloping St Katharine's Dock area. If these two wards are excluded, then the decline in the population of the remaining Docklands wards (a fall of 20.8 per cent) is much more dramatic and higher than the average for inner London. Apart from the western fringe, people were moving out of Docklands partly as a result of nineteenth-century housing being demolished and replaced by lower-density, often high-rise building, and partly as a response to the dramatic decline in jobs. The docks were running down with a declining volume of trade, and many closed. In addition, dock-related industries – food processing, transport, shipbuilding – were closing down so that people were being forced to look elsewhere in London for work. These two forces resulted in large population losses. Dockyard ward in Southwark lost nearly a third of its population (27.7 per cent) while the neighbouring ward of Riverside lost 19.6 per cent in the decade 1971–81. Further east, South ward in Newham lost 27.3 per cent of its population, 3,317 people, in absolute terms the largest population loss of any Docklands ward. Blackwall and Millwall at the heart of Docklands declined by 19.7 and 17.3 per cent respectively.

A demographic portrait from the 1981 Census of Population

The population of the eight Docklands wards was 68,765 in 1981, while that of the LDDC area was 38,310. The 1981 census coincides exactly with the creation of the LDDC and so it is possible to examine in detail the structure of the population at that date. For discussion here we can select only certain key indicators which highlight both the homogeneity of the area in some respects and its internal diversity in others. Thus, the indicators for

social class and housing reveal a high degree of uniformity in the area. But the demographic measures themselves show much more variety.

Social class
The homogeneity of social class within the Docklands is clearly shown by the social class of heads of households. Only in St Katharine's in the extreme west of the area was there a significant proportion of households headed by a non-manual worker: 32 per cent. Proportions of households with a head of household in manual work varied from 32 per cent in Riverside, to 58 per cent in South. Riverside's low proportion is explained by the large number (43 per cent) of households with a non-active head of household. The proportions aged 16 and over classified as skilled, semi-skilled and unskilled manual workers confirm the picture, with proportions varying from 36.8 per cent in St Katharine's to 64 per cent in South (table 10.2).

Housing tenure
The housing tenure of Docklands in 1981 was one of the most striking features of the area. In most part-wards, council ownership of housing was over 80 per cent, reaching over 90 per cent in St

Table 10.1   Population change 1971–81 for Docklands wards[1] and boroughs

Area	1971[2]	1981[2]	% change
Greater London	7,452,346	6,713,165	−9.9
Inner London	3,031,935	2,497,978	−7.6
Outer London	4,420,411	4,215,187	−4.6
Newham	237,390	209,494	−11.8
Custom House and			
Silvertown	12,876	11,161	−13.3
South	12,134	8,817	−27.3
Southwark	262,138	211,858	−19.2
Riverside	8,855	7,122	−19.6
Dockyard	11,198	8,102	−27.7
Tower Hamlets	165,776	142,841	−13.8
St Katharine's	10,360	10,161	−1.9
Shadwell	8,051	7,906	−1.8
Blackwall	6,848	5,498	−19.7
Millwall	12,094	9,998	−17.3

[1]Total ward population, including areas outside the LDDC zone
[2]Population present

Source: 1981 Census of Population

Katharine's, South and Riverside. Only in Custom House and Silvertown in Newham did the percentage fall to 68 per cent, still considerably higher than the inner London average. The only significant owner occupation was in this ward: 17.4 per cent, still a much lower proportion than in inner London as a whole. In every other part-ward the percentage of housing in owner occupation was below 5 per cent (table 10.2).

Age
The age structure reflects the varying economic and demographic processes at work among the Docklands wards in the 1970s: for example, earlier economic decline and out-migration in the Southwark wards, in-migration to Tower Hamlets and the relative stability of the indigenous population in Newham.

The three Docklands boroughs with between 19.7 per cent (Southwark) and 23.1 per cent (Newham) aged under 16 had a slightly more youthful population than inner London as a whole in 1981 (18.8 per cent aged under 16), comparable with Greater London's 20 per cent. But within the LDDC area the population was generally much

more youthful although there were considerable contrasts between the far-west part-wards, especially Riverside in Southwark with only 15.6 per cent under 16 and, further east in Newham, with South having a quarter aged under 16 and Custom House 27.5 per cent (table 10.2). Similarly, the proportions over retirement age within the three Docklands boroughs were generally fairly comparable with London as a whole (17.9 per cent) varying from 16.3 per cent in Newham to 18.7 per cent in Southwark. But the part-wards within the LDDC varied much more. Again, Riverside was the most divergent with nearly a quarter of its population over retirement age, while the others varied from a low of 11.3 per cent in Custom House (Newham) and 11.8 per cent in St Katharine's (Tower Hamlets) to 15.0 per cent in Dockyard (Southwark) (table 10.2).

Birthplace
The importance of immigration from abroad varies very significantly from place to place in Docklands. The percentage of residents born in the New Commonwealth and Pakistan was highest in Shadwell (17.4 per cent) followed by Blackwall and St Katharine's. These people form part of the

Table 10.2   Selected demographic characteristics of wards and part-wards within the LDDC area, 1981

Area	(1)	(2)	(3)	(4)	(5)	(6)	(7)	(8)	(9)
Newham									
Customhouse and Silvertown	27.5	11.3	14.1	52.2	51.9	17.4	68.0	6.4	11.2
South	25.0	13.5	9.0	58.2	64.0	0.6	92.4	4.9	8.4
Southwark									
Riverside	15.6	24.1	18.4	32.5	48.2	2.1	93.7	2.5	4.5
Dockyard	23.0	15.0	18.3	45.5	49.8	1.9	80.9	5.4	8.5
Tower Hamlets									
St Katharine's	19.3	11.8	32.0	45.6	36.8	2.3	90.7	12.3	18.5
Shadwell	22.9	13.7	15.9	43.9	46.2	3.7	80.7	17.4	27.9
Blackwall	23.6	13.6	14.8	49.3	45.1	2.5	87.5	13.3	21.6
Millwall	23.5	13.7	18.0	47.8	48.3	4.2	83.4	5.8	9.5

(1) % population aged under 16.
(2) % population aged over retirement age (Male 65, Females 60+)
(3) % of household heads in social classes I, II, IIIN (non-manual)
(4) % of household heads in social classes IIIM, IV, & V (manual)
(5) % employed residents, in skilled, semi-skilled and unskilled manual work.
(6) % of households in owner-occupied property.
(7) % of households in council-owned property.
(8) % of population born in New Commonwealth or Pakistan.
(9) % of population in households with head born in New Commonwealth or Pakistan.

Source: Census, small area statistics for part-wards, OPCS

high concentrations of migrants, from Bangladesh especially, in the western part of the borough of Tower Hamlets. Elsewhere percentages varied from 2.5 per cent in Riverside to 6.4 per cent in Custom House and Silvertown (table 10.2). In order to arrive at a more accurate estimate of the size of the ethnic minority population, including those people born in the UK to migrant parents, we may use the alternative measure of the population living in households whose head was born in the New Commonwealth or Pakistan. By this measure, Shadwell stood at 28 per cent, Blackwall at 22 per cent and St Katharine's at 18.5 per cent, reflecting the recency of the migration stream and the numbers born in the UK.

Household size and composition
Given the more youthful age-structure of the Docklands population in 1981 compared with inner London as a whole, it is not surprising that the proportion of one-person households was generally below the inner London average. Only in the western part of the area, in St Katharine's north of the river and Riverside to the south, were percentages near those of inner London (table 10.3). In Newham, Custom House had only 19.2 per cent one-person households, and South 22.2 per cent. Millwall was only a little higher with 23.2

per cent. Larger households of five or more showed considerable variation among the eight part-wards, ranging from 6.7 per cent in Riverside to 14.2 per cent in Shadwell (table 10.3).

Particular types of households give some indication of the needs that may be evident in particular areas. Both lone-parent households and pensioner households may have a greater level of need than those with at least two younger adults, and are particularly characteristic of inner-urban areas.

Lone-adult households with children under 16, with the exception of St Katharine's and Riverside, made up a higher proportion of households in the Docklands than for inner London generally (which itself had a much higher proportion of these households than nationally). In South ward, Newham, the proportions reached 7.3 per cent, twice the inner London average. Households with three or more dependent children are increasingly a minority group within society. In Docklands in 1981 proportions varied from only 4 per cent of households in Riverside and 5.8 per cent in St Katharine's, the only part wards below the London average of 6.4 per cent, to 10 per cent in Custom House and Silvertown. Lone-pensioner households

Table 10.3   Household size and composition for wards and part-wards in LDDC area, 1981

	(1)	(2)	(3)	(4)	(5)	(6)	(7)
Newham							
Customhouse and Silvertown	2.91	19.2	14.0	4.9	10.0	25.8	10.2
South	2.80	22.2	13.5	7.3	8.0	30.1	14.3
Southwark							
Riverside	2.35	30.1	6.7	2.8	4.0	25.3	21.5
Dockyard	2.52	26.4	9.0	5.6	6.7	31.3	15.8
Tower Hamlets							
St. Katharine's	2.42	30.7	8.9	2.8	5.8	23.3	12.1
Shadwell	2.65	28.4	14.2	4.1	9.1	27.6	14.1
Blackwall	2.65	27.3	13.1	5.3	9.4	28.9	13.8
Millwall	2.73	23.2	12.9	4.5	8.6	26.6	12.9

(1) Average household size
(2) % 1 person households
(3) % 5 person or more households
(4) % lone-adult households with child(ren) under 16
(5) % households with 3 or more dependent children
(6) % households with 1 or more pensioners
(7) % lone-pensioner households

Source: 1981 Census of Population unpublished data for wards.

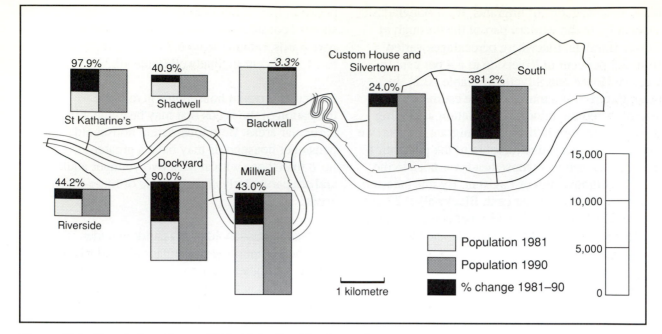

Figure 10.1 Population change 1981–90 for Docklands wards.
Source: Table 10.4

by contrast were below the inner London average of 15.8 per cent in all part-wards apart from Riverside, where 21.5 per cent of all households were lone pensioners. Indeed in Riverside, 45 per cent of all households contained at least one pensioner.

The population of the LDDC zone in 1981 therefore represented most of the classic features associated with inner-city decay. Even so, there was considerable variation within the area, related to the particular history of economic decline. We may see this variation at a more detailed scale still if we look at variations within wards, at the level of the census enumeration district (areas usually of between 200 and 500 people). In the case of Shadwell ward, for example, amongst its seven enumeration districts the proportion of one-person households varied from 16 per cent to 44 per cent, average household size from 2.2 to 3.3, and the proportion of the population living in households whose head was born in the New Commonwealth and Pakistan from 7 per cent to 48 per cent.

Population growth 1981–90 and projected growth to 2001

The London Docklands Household Survey (LDDC, 1991) allows us to be fairly clear about population trends during the 1980s. Table 10.4 and figure 10.1 show that an overall growth of some 60 per cent between 1981 and 1990 in the LDDC area was not spread uniformly: the greatest growth

occurred in South ward in Newham, Dockyard ward in Southwark and St Katharine's in Tower Hamlets. Nevertheless, substantial growth took place in all but one of the wards and is in marked contrast with the pattern of decline of the previous decade shown in table 10.1. Relative growth has been least in the Isle of Dogs, which has been dominated by commercial development in the Enterprise Zone.

The projections for borough populations have been made by the London Research Centre and in this discussion projected population change in the whole ward is necessarily discussed rather than just that part of the ward within the LDDC (table 10.5). In almost every case, these wards have a projected population growth that is totally divergent from the rest of the borough, in direct relation to the new housing projected for the wards as the development of Docklands continues to the end of the century. Indeed the population of the LDDC area is projected to comprise nearly 20 per cent of the population of the three boroughs by the year 2001 compared with only 7 per cent in 1981.

Newham
Within the borough of Newham it is the two Docklands wards of Custom House and Silvertown and South which have the only consistent projected population growth to the end of the century. Initially, between 1981 and 1991, South ward, which includes the Beckton area in the Royal Docks, had the highest rate of increase, while growth in Custom House and Silvertown was

Table 10.4   Population changes in wards and part-wards in the LDDC area, 1981–90

	1981[1]	% of ward	1990 population	% change 1981–90
Newham				
Custom House and Silvertown	7,411	67.0	9,192	24.0
South	1,869	21.2	8,993	381.2
Southwark				
Riverside	2,640	37.0	3,808	44.2
Dockyard	5,854	72.5	11,120	90.0
Tower Hamlets				
St Katharine's	3,006	31.2	5,949	97.9
Shadwell	2,145	27.1	3,022	40.9
Blackwall	5,399	98.3	5,223	*−3.3*
Millwall	9,986	100.0	14,275	43.0
Total	**38,310**	–	**61,582**	**60.7**

[1] Usually resident population

Source: 1981 Census of Population; London Docklands Household Survey (table 4)

lower. But between 1991 and 1996, population increase is projected to become much faster in Custom House and to slow down in South. The majority of the increase in Custom House is projected to be a result of in-migration. In all other Newham wards net out-migration is projected between 1996 and 2001, while in Custom House and Silvertown the population is expected to grow by a further 33 per cent, mainly as a result of in-migration, and in South by 7 per cent. The rest of the borough has a projected growth of only 1.7 per cent.

Southwark
The two Docklands wards of Dockyard and Riverside are again the only wards within the borough to show a consistent increase in projected population to the end of the century. Between 1981 and 1986, a large increase of 16 per cent and 23.5 per cent took place and this was projected to continue, with quinquennial increases of around 10 per cent in Riverside and 25 per cent in Dockyard up to the year 2001, with more than three-quarters of this increase a result of net in-migration. Elsewhere in the borough net out-migration is projected in almost all the wards. By 1996, these two wards are projected to have the highest proportions in the younger adult age group of any wards in Southwark.

Tower Hamlets
Between 1981 and 1986 the largest population increases in the borough were in Spitalfields (up by 15 per cent) rather than in the Docklands wards. St Katharine's was, however, the second fastest growing ward in Tower Hamlets (up by 12 per cent). The impact of redevelopment is shown by the contrasted structure of the growth. In Spitalfields 83 per cent of the growth was a result of natural increase, while in St Katharine's, 33 per cent of the growth was a result of in-migration, the former associated in part with the high fertility and young age-structure of the ethnic minority population, and the latter with the arrival of new residents in the redeveloped areas.

Elsewhere, the Docklands wards showed the beginnings of growth in contrast to the population losses of the 1970s. The projections for 1991–96 continue the trend of growth in the 1980s: increases of 8 per cent (Blackwall), 12 per cent (Millwall) and 15 per cent (St Katharine's), and in each case around 40 per cent of the growth a result of in-migration. The picture continues to 2001 with similar rates of increase projected for these wards.

Finally, we should note that the economic and housing slump in Docklands from late 1988, with housing proving difficult to sell, and new projects being abandoned, may mean that the population projections may be achieved more slowly.

Who are the new Docklands residents?

The characteristics of the new residents in Docklands are far from uniform. Whilst to some extent they do fit the image of a new middle-class élite much vaunted in the media and by those trying to 'sell' the area, they also reflect the fact that new housing developments vary considerably amongst the four zones. Thus, KFR Research (1987) show that both the type of housing and its price vary from a predominance of plush warehouse conversions in Wapping and Limehouse, to newly built blocks of high-status flats in the Isle of Dogs, to smaller-scale housing developments in the Royals in the east. There is considerable variety within most zones although, as chapter 8 discusses in detail, the great majority of newly built or converted property is in the private sector.

Again, the Docklands Household Survey reveals the dramatic changes in the population structure between 1981 and 1990. As well as a rise in the total population, there was also a disproportionately rapid rise in the number of households (up by 74%). Average household size

has declined to 2.41, a sharp contrast with 1981 (table 10.3). This was in part the result of the arrival in the area of a large number of young one- and two-person households. Figure 10.2 shows that the age-groups 25–39 experienced by far the largest increase. In Newham and Southwark it trebled, in Tower Hamlets it doubled. We should also note the very high degree of residential mobility: over two-thirds of all individuals living in their current address in Docklands have moved into or within the area since 1980. Finally, the survey points to the very important changes in the sorts of property ownership amongst residents. As chapter 8 showed, there has been a massive increase in owner-occupation and a decline in the relative importance of local authority housing, though in absolute terms the latter has declined relatively little. There has also been a considerable increase in housing association and privately rented accommodation.

It is in one area, of Wapping and Limehouse (which are part of the wards of St Katharine's and Shadwell shown in fig. 10.1) that we may be more specific still about the demographic and other characteristics of new arrivals. This is an area where development is at a more advanced stage than elsewhere in Docklands: it was estimated that by early 1989 some 43 per cent of potential

Table 10.5 Projected populations of wards, of which all or part lie within LDDC area

	1981[1]	1981–86 % change	1986	1986–91 % change	1991	1991–96 % change	1996	1996–2001 % change	2001
Newham									
Custom House and									
Silvertown	11,253	3.03	10,833	6.6	11,548	34.0	15,479	32.8	20,555
South	8,985	9.04	8,019	19.2	16,605	8.0	17,941	6.8	19,153
Southwark									
Riverside	7,424	15.95	8,608	10.7	9,529	11.8	10,656	9.9	11,706
Dockyard	8,408	23.52	10,386	22.5	12,726	27.2	16,182	24.9	20,213
Tower Hamlets									
St Katharine's	9,990	12.2	11,212	23.9	13,892	14.6	15,923	14.8	18,278
Shadwell	8,203	6.7	8,755	5.8	9,263	4.3	9,568	4.4	10,084
Blackwall	5,696	4.0	5,924	13.1	6,697	8.2	7,249	8.4	7,858
Millwall	10,356	7.9	11,172	19.1	13,310	11.9	14,898	12.1	16,699

[1] These differ from census figures since they are mid year estimates

Source: London Research Centre: 1981 figures are base populations of wards taken from table 2 of SAS adjusted upwards to 1981 mid year estimates; 1986 ward estimates of population are controlled to an LRC borough estimate of resident population; 1991 and after figures: projection 1 – assumption of high fertility after 1988 and up to 2001; plus dwelling-led migration (dwelling stock forecasts supplied by individual London boroughs).

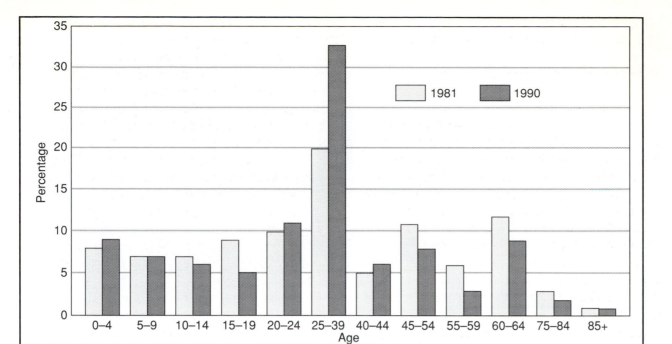

Figure 10.2 Percentage distribution of the population in the LDDC area by age in 1990 compared to 1981.
Source: London Docklands Housing Survey (1991), p.43

residential development in the area would have been completed (KFR Research, 1987). A recent questionnaire survey carried out by the Department of Geography at Queen Mary and Westfield College revealed that some 38 per cent of new households were single-person and a further 45 per cent were two-person. Only 7 per cent of the population in households who had arrived since 1981 were children under the age of 15. The great majority of the new residents were single people or couples between the ages of 21 and 40 (some 61 per cent), the modal age-group being the 26–30-year-olds. There were more men than women, particularly amongst the single-person households where two-thirds were men. Only 15 per cent of new arrivals were aged over 50. These age data reflect the picture shown by the first housing survey on purchasers of new houses carried out by the LDDC. This showed that 60 per cent of the occupants in the sample were aged between 21 and 30 and only 2 per cent were aged over 50 (LDDC 1987, p. 68). The marketing strategies discussed in chapter 4 clearly had their effect.

Further points of interest in the survey also contrast sharply with the profile of the area in 1981. Thus, of the principal respondents to the survey, only 3 per cent were born in the three Dockland boroughs. A further 25 per cent were born elsewhere in London. Some 21 per cent were born outside the UK, but with strong representation from other parts of Europe and the developed world generally, rather than from the Third World. In terms of

mobility within the UK (table 10.6), the survey indicates that the Docklands had rapidly become part of the general London housing market. Some 60 per cent of new residents had their last place of residence in London, and a further 18 per cent within the rest of south-east England. Indeed, there is already evidence of movement within the Docklands area: some 27 per cent listed their previous place of residence within the three boroughs, usually indicating a move up-market within the area. That these are not 'locals' moving into the new housing is confirmed by the birthplace data and, given the price of property, this is scarcely surprising. Finally, it is worth noting that

Table 10.6 Place of birth and last previous place of residence of new residents in Wapping

Area	Place of birth %	Place of last previous residence %
Three Dockland boroughs	3.2	27.1
Rest of east London	1.0	3.4
Rest of London	23.8	29.5
South East England	17.5	17.9
Rest of UK	33.7	10.9
Elsewhere Europe	7.0	4.7
Outside Europe	13.8	6.5
	100.0	100.0

Source: Crilley, Bryce, Hall and Ogden (1991)

Photo: Philip Ogden

View from the south bank over to the Wapping riverside where survey work amongst new residents, reported here, was undertaken.

some 11 per cent of our respondents gave their last place of residence as outside the UK. Overall, the new residents showed a high level of residential mobility, with a number of previous places of residence before Docklands.

A key motive for many new arrivals was convenience for work: some 29 per cent worked in the City of London, a further 13 per cent within Docklands and almost all the rest elsewhere in London. Some 55 per cent gave convenience as their first choice when asked to name the reasons for moving to the area.

In another sense too this is a highly mobile population: data relating to the first respondent in the survey does show the existence of an international salariat moving frequently between the world's business centres . Although for the majority London was the base for their activities, 18 per cent worked for organisations with headquarters located in either Europe or the USA. More than one-quarter of respondents indicated that they had visited Europe at least once for business in the previous twelve months and more than half this group had made two or more visits. In the previous twelve months 15 per cent had visited America. A related indicator, which again could scarcely be in greater contrast to the characteristics of 1981 residents, is the prevalence of second-home ownership: for some 14.4 per cent

their Docklands residence was merely a *pied-à-terre* and a further 8.4 per cent had their main home in London and a second home elsewhere. These various characteristics are in line with income figures. Of the respondents 66 per cent were earning over £20,000 per annum in 1990 and 29 per cent over £40,000. Household incomes were generally much higher than this, since many had two principal earners. Nearly 90 per cent of respondents were in professional occupations including 26 per cent in financial services. In addition, educational qualifications were very high, with 55 per cent of first respondents having a first or higher degree.

The arrival of new residents is therefore a crucial ingredient in the social and economic transformation of the area. Relatively few residents who lived in the area prior to 1981 have been resettled or directly displaced by new development (exceptions are for the Limehouse Link road and for various housing agreements between local authorities and the LDDC). It should also be re-emphasised that the new housing market in Docklands is more varied than is sometimes suggested. The evidence from Wapping represents one part of the story, but more research is needed into the new residential population of the Surrey Docks, the Isle of Dogs or Beckton in order to clarify the workings of the local housing market.

11 The architectural expression

Matthew Saunders

Stephanie Williams begins her 1990 guide to Docklands with the provocative assertion that 'London's Docklands contains one of the worst collections of late twentieth century building to be seen anywhere in the world'. She redresses the balance later by admitting that the area also has 'some of the best British architecture of the 1980s'. Hers is a very widely accepted perception, common within the architectural profession as well as amongst the general public.

Architecture, planning and the LDDC

Disappointment with the majority of buildings, highlighted by the critical acclaim accorded to the few, is blamed very largely on the hectic pace at which Docklands has 'taken off', reduced interference from the 'planners' and, indeed, the lack of any attempt at comprehensive planning. Because of the way development was encouraged, there was little attempt to regulate land-use or architectural style for the LDDC area as a whole. This is in sharp contrast to past practice in, for example, the New Towns.

In the determination of applications on listed buildings and Conservation Areas, the LDDC is for the most part autonomous, being free from direction either by English Heritage (which otherwise has the power of veto on listed building consents throughout London) or by the local authority although consultations with both are common practice. The more important cases, for example London Bridge City, have been 'called in' by the Secretary of State for determination after a Public Inquiry. Generally, the LDDC has seen its job in established areas as development rather than redevelopment. When compared with the dock companies that preceded it, remembering that 1100 houses, a hospital and a church had to be destroyed to make way for St Katharine's Docks near the Tower of London in 1828, it is remarkably conservative both in its planning regime and its subsidy: £250,000 of LDDC money has gone to the repair of St Matthias, Poplar, built in the mid seventeenth century as the private chapel to the East India Dock Company; £330,000 to St Anne's Limehouse, one of Hawksmoor's great Baroque churches of the early eighteenth century; and £240,000 to the early nineteenth century All Saints, Poplar, mainly to bring its crypt into community use. A number of museums would not have started but for LDDC financial support. General planning controls where conservation interests are not affected are exercised by the LDDC alone except in exceptional cases, whilst in the Enterprise Zone declared in 1982 in the centre of the Isle of Dogs there are virtually no planning controls at all. As with the end of literary censorship in the 1960s, some architects and clients alike exploited the new licence by providing purely utilitarian or gimmicky structures, several of them to prove short-lived. A greater maturity is now being shown. Canary Wharf, for example, has been conceived on a grand scale, sharpening the contrast with the surrounding jumble of buildings on the Isle of Dogs.

The epitome of Post-Modernism?

The LDDC controls just 21 square kilometres. Even so, its development plans, for example for 34,000 homes by the year 2000 of which half have so far been built or started (chapter 8), represent one of the greatest building campaigns underway in western Europe. And yet there is no hermetic seal dividing it from London or the country as a whole, and a lot of the professional criticism of the Docklands comes from those who lambast it for expressing in its rawest form the national success of Post-Modernism.

Post-Modernism is a term adopted for architectural polemics by the American-born writer Charles Jencks in 1975. It is architecture that self-consciously rejects the severity and rectilinearity of the products of the Modern Movement, that borrows freely from the repertoire of architectural motifs from the past, loves colour and is not afraid of populism. In the nineteenth century, the architectural profession was divided between the Classicists and the Goths; nowadays the gulf is

Photo: LDDC

Docklands Light Railway poster highlighting John Outram's pumping station on the Isle of Dogs.

Photo: LDDC

China Wharf on the south bank of the Thames: new flats adjacent to warehouse conversions.

between Post-Modern and High-Tech, the latter epitomised by Richard Rogers' Lloyds Building in the City. Here excitement comes from showing how the building works and self-consciously exploiting the visual potential of undisguised technology.

There are High-Tech buildings in the Docklands: Nicholas Grimshaw's Printing Works of 1988 for *The Financial Times* at 240 East India Dock Road, (see p. 47) exposes printing machinery through a sheer glass wall atmospherically illuminated at night; the Design Museum in Butler's Wharf off Shad Thames, converted by Conran Roche from a warehouse of the 1950s, is a pure echo of the 'white liner' style beloved of the early pre-War Modernists. Nevertheless, think of Docklands and you think of Post-Modernism, so that those who tend to dismiss the latter as superficial, flashy and transitory damn the LDDC as one of its main progenitors. For many the controversy over the London Bridge City site immediately adjacent to Tower Bridge summed up the moral relativism of Post-Modernism – the developer offered three dramatically contrasting schemes in the hope that

Photo: Matthew Saunders

A back view of Butler's Wharf, recently converted to residential use.

one would get through the planning mill: a straightforward commercial scheme, a lame echo of the Palace of Westminster by the American architect Philip Johnson, and a rather more self-confident and full-blooded version of the area around the Doge's Palace in Venice by the young Classicist, John Simpson. Simpson won but nothing has so far happened on site.

Antecedents

The LDDC reflects not just the architectural manners of its day but even more so the *laissez-faire*, free-market thinking of Margaret Thatcher's first government. But that ethos is not all-pervasive. Its missionary zeal, its conscious advocacy of 'good architecture' and its lately developed pursuit of a socially rounded community all have pre-Thatcherite antecedents. The East End has seen many attempts to redress its poverty over the centuries, much of it religiously directed. Hawksmoor's six great Baroque churches of the early eighteenth century were built primarily to serve the middle classes of the area but the so-called Waterloo Churches (including St Paul's, Shadwell, of 1818, and St James's, Bermondsey, of 1827) were constructed under the Church Building Act of 1818, which set aside £1 million to provide new churches throughout the country both to 'Church' the masses and counter the spread of Nonconformity. The several missions and university settlements set up from the mid nineteenth century by all denominations from Quakers to Catholics combined social purpose (as in the dispensaries to provide medical and surgical help to the poor) with the desire to improve the area through the provision of architectural flagships. Canon Samuel Barnett, founder of Toynbee Hall in 1888, believed in addressing the whole person, physical and spiritual, feeding his flock, educating them and giving them, whether they wanted it or not, the Whitechapel Picture Exhibition. Other philanthropists such as George Peabody, the American-born banker, and Sir Sidney Waterlow established model housing, whilst Baroness Burdett-Coutts' majestic Gothic Columbia Market building at Bethnal Green (now demolished) gave the poor access to cheap food and architectural grandeur. The pattern was followed in our own century with the pioneering work of Dr Alfred Salter, a Quaker MP and GP, who sponsored the minute Garden City centred on Wilson Grove in Bermondsey (now a Conservation Area), and by the Lansbury Estate in Poplar, north of the East India Dock Road, built for the Festival of Britain in 1951 as a 'Live Architecture' exhibit.

The combination in the LDDC of strong public authority with active encouragement of private endeavour echoes many of these historical strands. The LDDC is clearly a successor to the New Town Corporations established in 1946, whilst reliance on the developer to contribute to the transport infrastructure, as in Olympia and York's support for the Light Transit Railway (LTR) extension to the City of London, has distant but direct echoes in the joint venture of the West India and London Dock Companies in the construction of Commercial Road in 1806 to link the East India Docks with the Company's warehouses in the City. The New Town Corporations used the best designers and acted as a natural milieu for architects with views on the left. The LDDC's first Chief Architect and Planner until he left in 1985, Edward Hollamby, brought with him not just socialist convictions, but his ownership of William Morris's Red House at Bexleyheath. For him the LDDC began as a great social and architectural crusade. The problem has been that the method chosen for regeneration – the free market – has been in tension, creative and otherwise, with the notion of comprehensive planning.

Conservation

The conservation of old buildings has been a central part of the creation of a new image of Docklands, actively encouraged by the LDDC. For example, in trying to attract a new residential population, historical associations with the River Thames and the port, expressed through the renovation of old buildings, have played a vital role.

Conservation controls have increased under the LDDC. By 1991 there were eighteen Conservation Areas, in which demolition of buildings and felling of trees are controlled and schemes of enhancement encouraged, whilst the LDDC urged the Department of the Environment to update the inventory of listed buildings in its area, which it did by 1983, raising the total to over 500. Thenceforward, the great mass of surviving nineteenth-century warehousing became listed, as did many examples of the more idiosyncratic structures which give Docklands its particular character, including cranes and the hydraulic pumping station at Wapping (listed in the second-highest category Grade II*). A secondary 'local' list has been compiled to identify structures not quite good enough for listing but worthy of protection if circumstances permit.

It is true that the LDDC has itself backed applications to demolish listed buildings, as with the Anning and Chadwick Warehouse on the site of London Bridge City, and the W11 Warehouse at Butler's Wharf, but in both cases their viewpoint was upheld in the subsequent decision by the Department of the Environment to grant consent.

The quintessential building type of the Docklands is of course the warehouse, a structure which lent itself more readily to adaptation than many others. It had been built to a high loadbearing capacity with uncluttered floorspace and with an eye to the prevention of fire. These advantages, combined with the proximity of many warehouses to the river, meant that the developers needed little encouragement, especially after the founding of the LDDC, to convert them to flats and offices. To Derek Jarman, the film producer, his spartan warehouse of the 1970s was the equivalent of the garret of the starving artist, but the average resident is now the professional, the young and the well-to-do (chapter 10). It has often proved possible to maintain the ruggedly severe character of the exterior (although many developers have insisted upon the addition of balconies from where the river views can be enjoyed), whilst internally the cast-iron columns, after coating with intumescent paint, acquire the necessary fire resistance that permits their retention. Several warehouses still have the constant smell of the spices that used to be stored there, the timbers having been impregnated with it. In the street known as Shad Thames on the South Bank just by Tower Bridge, the brooding cliff-like facades on either side, including the dramatic crisscross of wrought iron gantries, have lost none of that 'Dickensian' appeal.

Commerical uses can be more difficult to insert: a large glass screen is proposed in the end of the greatest stretch of unconverted warehouses, the West India Dock of 1800–02, designed by Gwilt and built by William Adam, with the earliest use of cast-iron windows in a warehouse – in a scheme by architects Feilden and Mawson for shops and offices. At the Skin Floor (now known as Tobacco Dock), built in London Docks between 1811 and 1814 to the designs of Daniel Asher Alexander, architect, and John Rennie, engineer, fire

regulations demanded the removal of substantial sections of the roof to create fire breaks. The result has achieved dramatic spatial effects increased by the scooping out of huge matching 'eyes' in the vaults of the lower floor. These 'interventions' in the scheme for retail conversion devised by Terry Farrell are unabashed, but the critical consensus has it that this extraordinary building constructed to house tobacco on the ground floor where the roof is supported by cast-iron trees, with wine and brandy in the vaults beneath, is the great conservation success of the Docklands. Sadly, this has not been reflected commercially.

Self-conscious 'interventions' have also dramatised the development of shops and offices known as Hays Galleria on the South Bank at Bermondsey. Here a great curved barrel vault in welded steel, running from the river, shelters the shoppers as they patronise the units created on the ground floor of two matching warehouses of 1861.

New buildings

In turning to new buildings, we find that some of the more obviously prestigious projects have been architecturally disappointing. The £40 million headquarters of News International, known colloquially as 'Fortress Wapping', presents the most uninviting exterior of any building in Docklands. The Docklands Light Railway, begun in 1984, is largely functional in its architectural expression, although the 120-foot span over the station at Canary Wharf is impressive. The £30 million spent on the Airport clearly did not go on providing a building of memorable architectural character. The new Billingsgate Market on the Isle of Dogs will never be listed like its original in the City.

A regular stream of visitors is finding its way to Stewart Street in the Isle of Dogs to experience the exotic design by John Outram for a pumping station commissioned directly by the LDDC (see p. 82). The polychromatic brick banding, the huge schematic, vividly painted capitals, and the central fan in the pediment looking like the propeller of a plane, provide a building with many rich historical and functional references. Even though finished only in 1988, it has already become a design classic.

Also completed in 1988 and equally novel in its form is the £18 million tower block of 171 flats in

Westferry Road, E14, known as 'Cascades'. Designed by Campbell, Zogolovitch, Wilkinson and Gough (CZWG), the name comes from the great slide at one side, but the leitmotifs of the designers comes out, too, in the variety of windows and balconies and the polychromy. The same designers were behind the even more arresting 'Circle' in Queen Elizabeth Street, SE1, finished in 1990 after the expenditure of £32 million. It is, again as the name implies, a giant circle of separate blocks faced in rich blue tiles with balconies riding up the facades at a diagonal. Their China Wharf (1988) (see p.82) presents a striking Expressionist elevation to the river. Other architectural practices do not strive so much for effect. The housing by Jeremy Dixon at Compass Point on the Isle of Dogs (admired by the Prince of Wales), and that at Shadwell Basin by MacCormac, Jamieson, Pritchard and Wright, combine a humanity of scale with lightly displayed historical resonances. Julyan Wickham's Horselydown Square, just off Shad Thames, begun in 1987, is a richly modelled newcomer in a historically sensitive area and the nearby David Mellor Building of 1990 by Michael Hopkins combines a purity of form with excellence of execution. Troughton McAslan's riverside building in Elephant Lane, Rotherhithe is clearly directly inspired by historic Modernism from between the wars.

Canary Wharf

The complex which will undoubtedly come to symbolise Docklands in achitecture, as in other matters, is Canary Wharf on the Isle of Dogs. Despite its size and the impact on the famous view from Greenwich Palace, it was granted planning permission without a Public Inquiry. Its sponsors intended it to rival the City of London with which it is connected through the DLR extension to Bank. The 800-foot high tower dominating the 71-acre site and faced in stainless steel (where some of the lower offices are given a cladding in reconstituted limestone) is the tallest office block in the United Kingdom (although not in Europe, that record being taken by a structure in Frankfurt). The authorship of the complex is mixed, but the tower comes from the pen of Cesar Pelli, the Argentinian-born architect famous for his skyscrapers in America. The project will cost a breathtaking £4 billion. At the time of writing, the complex was still incomplete, although it is now possible to gauge the majesterial scale and ambition. The tower dominates from afar but, close to, it is the varied and rich detailing of the lower blocks and the landscaping with trees and commissions overseen by Sir Roy Strong that commands attention.

By the time the LDDC is dissolved in 1996, it will have left as its legacy the greatest concentration of building activity seen in London since the Second World War. In retrospect, 1990–92 will no doubt be seen as the period of stagnation, for Docklands suffered more than most from the recession but, more than any other of the Urban Development Corporations, it has managed to foster some memorable new designs as well as conservation successes. The great drawback is that individual successes have not been integrated into any wider planning framework and their effect is contradicted by much mediocrity. The LDDC's sister on Merseyside, admittedly dramatically less supported financially by the DoE, has the reinvigoration of Albert Docks, the largest complex of Grade I listed warehouses of the 1840s in the country, as the greatest feather in its cap, but little of the new design it has promoted will be remembered. That at least cannot be said about the LDDC.

Bibliography and further reading

This list contains all items to which reference is made in the book, along with other background references. The items most suitable for follow-up reading are marked with an asterisk.

* Al Naib S. K. (1986) **Dockland. An Illustrated Historical Survey of Life and Work in East London** North East London Polytechnic, London

* Al Naib S. K. (1990) **London Docklands: Past, Present and Future** Ashmead Press, London

* Ambrose P. (1986) **Whatever Happened to Planning?** Methuen, London, especially chapter 8, pp. 214–53

Anderson J. (1990) The 'new right', Enterprise Zones and Urban Development Corporations **International Journal of Urban and Regional Research**, 14, 3, pp. 468–89

Architectural Review (1989) 'Dockland development', 95, 1106, pp. 27–88

* Association of London Authorities and Docklands Consultative Committee (1991) **10 Years of Docklands: How the Cake was Cut** ALA and DCC, London

Batley R. (1989) 'London Docklands: an analysis of power relations between UDCs and local government' **Public Administration** 67, pp. 167–87

BIS (Bank for International Settlements) (1991) 'Capital flows in the 1980s: a survey of major trends' **BIS Economic Paper, 30** BIS, Basle

* Brindley T., Y. Rydin and G. Stoker (1989) **Remaking Planning. The Politics of Urban Change in the Thatcher Years** Unwin Hyman, London, especially chapter 6, pp. 96–120

* Brownill S. (1990) **Developing London's Docklands. Another Great Planning Disaster?** Paul Chapman, London

* Budd L. and S. Whimster (1992, eds.) **Global Finance and Urban Living: a Study of Metropolitan Change** Routledge, London

Burgess J. (1986) 'Community organisations', in H. Clout, and P. Wood, (eds.) **London: Problems of Change** Longman, Harlow, pp. 160–67

Burgess J. and P. Wood (1988) 'Decoding Docklands. Place advertising and decision-making strategies of the small firm', in J. Eyles and D. M. Smith **Qualitative Methods in Geography** Polity Press, Cambridge, pp. 94–117

Byrne T. and D. J. Kostin (1990) **London Office Market II: Breaking the Code** New York, Salomon Brothers

Calvocoressi P. (1990) **Conservation in Dockland. Old buildings in a Changing Environment** Docklands Forum, London

Cassell M. (1991) 'Brakes go on a property boom' **The Financial Times**, 1 July

* Church A. (1988a) 'Urban regeneration in London's Docklands: a five-year policy review', **Environment and Planning C: Government and Policy** 6, pp. 187–208

Church A. (1988b) 'Demand-led planning, the inner city crisis and the labour market: London Docklands evaluated', in B. S. Hoyle, D. A. Pinder and M. S. Husain (eds.) **Revitalising the Waterfront: International Dimensions of Waterfront Redevelopment** Belhaven Press, London, pp. 199–221

Church A. and P. Ainley (1987) 'Inner city decline and regeneration: young people and the labour market in London's Docklands', in P. Brown and D. N. Ashton (eds.) **Education, Unemployment and Labour Markets** Falmer Press, London, pp. 71–92

* Church A. and J. M. Hall (1986) 'Discovery of Docklands' **Geographical Magazine** 58, 12, pp. 632–40

* Church A. and J. M. Hall (1989) 'Local initiatives for urban regeneration', in D.T. Herbert and D.M. Smith (eds.) **Social Problems and the City** OUP, Oxford, pp. 345–69

* Colenutt Bob (1991) 'The London Docklands Development Corporation: Has the community benefited?' in M. Keith and A. Rogers (eds.) **Hollow Promises. Rhetoric and Reality in the Inner City** Mansell, London, pp. 31–41

Congdon P. (1989) 'An analysis of population and social change in London wards in the 1980s', **Transactions, Institute of British Geographers** NS 14, pp. 478–91

Coupland A. (1989) 'Docklands' house prices', in DCC (Docklands Consultative Committee) **Priced Out of Town** DCC, London

CRDD (Campaign to Restore Democracy in Docklands) (1983) **Docklands Fights Back: Eighteen Months of the LDDC** Joint Docklands Action Group, London

Crilley D. (1990) 'The disorder of John Short's new urban order' **Transactions, Institute of British Geographers**, NS 15, pp. 232–38

Crilley D., C. Bryce, R. Hall and P. E. Ogden (1991) **New Migrants in London's Docklands** Research Paper 5, Department of Geography, Queen Mary and Westfield College, University of London

* DCC (Docklands Consultative Committee) (1988) **Urban Development Corporations. Six Years in London's Docklands** DCC, London

* DCC (Docklands Consultative Committee) (1990) **The Docklands Experiment. A Critical Review of Eight Years of the London Docklands Development Corporation** DCC, London

* DCC (Docklands Consultative Committee) (1991) **East London's Commercial Property Market Trends** DCC, London

Department of the Environment (1990) **Enterprise Zone Information 1987–88** HMSO, London

Department of Transport and London Docklands Development Corporation (1991) **London Docklands Transport: The Growing Network for the 1990s** DTp and LDDC, London

Dicken P. (1992) **Global Shift, The Internationalisation of Economic Activity** Paul Chapman, London, 2nd edn, chapter 11

Docklands Forum and Birkbeck College (1990) **Employment in Docklands** Docklands Forum and Birkbeck College, University of London, London

* Ellmers C. and A. Werner (1991) **Dockland Life. A Pictorial History of London's Docks 1860–1970** Mainstream Publishing and Museum of London, Edinburgh and London

Employment Committee (1988) **The Employment Effects of the UDCs** House of Commons Employment Committee, Third Report HC 327-1 and 327-11, HMSO, London

Fishman W.J. (1988) **East End 1888. A Year in a London Borough Among the Labouring Poor** Duckworth, London

* Fishman W. J., N. Breach and J. M. Hall (1990) **East End and Docklands** Duckworth, London

Frost M. E. (1991) 'Changes in economic structure and opportunity' in K. Hoggart and D. R. Green (eds.) **London. A New Metropolitan Geography** Edward Arnold, London, pp. 34–50

Goodwin M. (1991) 'Replacing a surplus population: the policies of the London Docklands Development Corporation', in J. Allen and C. Hamnett (eds.) **Housing and Labour Markets. Building the Connections** Unwin Hyman, London, pp. 254–75

Greater London Council (1983) **The East London File** GLC, London

Hall J. M. (1990a) **Metropolis Now! London and its Region** CUP, Cambridge

Hall J. M. (1990b) 'Docklands', in W. J. Fishman, N. Breach and J.M. Hall **East End and Docklands** Duckworth, London, pp. 51–9

* Hall P. (1988) **Cities of Tomorrow** Blackwell, Oxford, pp. 343–61

* Hardy D. (1983a) 'Making sense of London Docklands: processes of change' **Papers in Geography and Planning No. 9** Middlesex Polytechnic, Enfield

* Hardy D. (1983b) 'Making sense of London Docklands: people and places' **Papers in Geography and Planning No. 10** Middlesex Polytechnic, Enfield

Hardy D. (1991) 'Transforming London Docklands', letter to **The Times** 12 September, p.17

Harvey D. (1978) 'The urban process under capitalism. A framework for analysis' **International Journal of Urban and Regional Research** 2, 1, pp. 101–31

Harvey D. (1985) **The Urbanization of Capital** Basil Blackwell, Oxford

Harvey D. (1989a) 'Down towns', **Marxism Today** p. 21

Harvey D. (1989b) **The Condition of Post-Modernity. An Enquiry into the Origins of Cultural Change** Blackwell, Oxford

Henley Centre (1990) **London 2000** Prepared for the Association of London Authorities

Hoggart K. and D. R. Green (eds.) (1991) **London. A New Metropolitan Geography** Edward Arnold, London

Hollamby T. (1990) **Dockland: London's Backyard into Frontyard** Docklands Forum, London

Hollamby T. and P. Da Luz (1988) 'Londres ouvre ses Docklands à l'investissement privé' **Urba** 225, pp. 12–21

Hostettler E. (1986) 'A Dockland community: the Isle of Dogs', in R. J. M. Carr (ed.) **Dockland: An Illustrated Historical Survey** GLC and North East London Polytechnic, London, pp. 59–70

Houlder V. (1990) 'A deep malaise which may take years to cure' **The Financial Times** 29 October

Houlder V. (1991a) 'London office vacancies at record, say surveyors' **The Financial Times** 10 June

Houlder V. (1991b) 'Safe haven sought for Docklands' **The Financial Times** 14 October

Houlder V. (1992a) 'London office glut worsens' **The Financial Times** 27 May

Houlder V. (1992b) 'A price on its high-rise head' **The Financial Times** 5 June

House of Commons (1987/88) **Third Report: the Employment Effects of Urban Development Corporations** Employment Committee, session 1987–88 HMSO, London

House of Commons (1988/89) **Twentieth Report: Urban Development Corporations** Committee of Public Accounts, session 1988–89, HC 385, HMSO, London

House of Lords (1981) Debate on the LDDC (Area and Constitution) Order, in **Lords Hansard** 1 July, cols. 194–204 and 213–35

House of Lords Select Committee on the LDDC (Area and Constitution Order) (1981) **Report** HMSO, London

Howick C. and T. Key (1978) **The Local Economy of Tower Hamlets: An Inner City Profile** Research Series 26, Centre for Environmental Studies, London

Hoyle B. S., D. A. Pinder and M. S. Husain (eds.) (1988) **Revitalising the Waterfront: International Dimensions of Waterfront Redevelopment** Belhaven Press, London

Jones Lang Wootton (1989) **London Docklands Review 1989** JLW, London

KFR Research (1987) **Docklands Commercial and Residential Developments** Knight, Frank and Rutley, London

King A. (1990) **Global Cities. Post-Imperialism and the Internationalization of London** Routledge, London

Lacey R. (1986) **Ford. The Men and the Machine** William Heinemann, London

Lawless P. (1989) **Britain's Inner Cities** Paul Chapman, London, 2nd edn

LDDC (1987) **Corporate Plan** LDDC, London

LDDC (1988a) **Annual Review 1987/1988** LDDC, London

LDDC (1988b) **Central Index of Statistics** LDDC, London

LDDC (1989) **Housing Strategy Review** LDDC, London

LDDC (1990) **Annual Review 1989/1990** LDDC, London

LDDC (1991a) **Corporate Plan** LDDC, London

LDDC (1991b) **The London Docklands Household Survey** LDDC, London

Ledgerwood G. (1985) **Urban Innovation: The Transformation of London's Docklands, 1968–84** Gower, Aldershot

Lee R. (1989) 'Social relations and the geography of material life', in D. Gregory and R. Walford (eds.) **Horizons in Human Geography** Macmillan, London, pp. 152–69

Local Economic Policy Unit (1991) **A Labour Market Strategy for Hackney, Islington and the City of London** London

London Borough of Newham (1991) **Newham's Royal Docklands: Vision for 2005** London Borough of Newham, London

London Borough of Tower Hamlets (1988) **A Study in the Economy of the Isle of Dogs** Isle of Dogs Neighbourhood Committee, Tower Hamlets, London

London Chamber of Commerce (1989) **Employment in Finance and Business Services: Trends and Prospects** London Economy Research Programme, LCC, London

London Research Centre (1987) **Docklands Housing Needs** LRC, London

McCallum J. (1991) 'End of controls provides a lift' **The Financial Times** 11 November

Marcan P. (1986) **Down in the East End. An Illustrated Anthology** Peter Marcan Publishers, London

Massey D. (1982) 'Enterprise zones: a political issue' **International Journal of Urban and Regional Research** 6, pp. 429–34

* Massey D. (1991) **Docklands. A Microcosm of Broader Social and Economic Trends** Docklands Forum, London

Mikardo I. (1990) **Docklands Redevelopment. How They Got It Wrong** Docklands Forum, London

Monahan P. (1989) **Guide to the London Docklands** William Curtis, London

Nairne S. (1987) **State of the Art** Jonathan Cape, London

National Audit Office (1988) **Department of the Environment: Urban Development Corporations**, HC 492, HMSO, London

* Nicholson R. (1988) **London Docklands. Street Atlas and Guide** Robert Nicholson Publications, London

Olympia & York (1991) **Canary Wharf Update** Olympia & York, London

Open University (1982) **Social Change, Geography and Policy** Course D102, Block 6, unit 23 (on the history of the East End); unit 24 (policy issues) and unit 25 (on the future of the Docklands), Open University, Milton Keynes

Page J. (1989) 'Tourism and accommodation in London: alternative policies and the London docklands experience' **Built Environment** 15, 2, pp. 125–37

Palmer A. (1989) **The East End: Four Centuries of London Life** John Murray, London

Public Accounts Committee, House of Commons (1989) **Urban Development Corporations** Twentieth Report, session 1988–89, HC 385, HMSO, London

Rajan A. and J. Fryatt (1988) **Create or Abdicate: The City's Human Resource Choice for the 1980s** Witherby, London

Richman G. (1975) **Fly a Flag for Poplar** Liberation Films, London

RISUL (1988) **LDDC Census of Employment 1987** Research International Specialist Units Ltd, LDDC, London

Robson B. (1988) **Those Inner Cities** OUP, Oxford

Rowthorn B. (1986) 'De-industrialisation in Britain', in R. Martin and B. Rowthorn **The Geography of De-industrialisation** Macmillan, London, pp. 1–30

Rowthorn R. E. and J. R. Wells (1987) **De-industrialization and Foreign Trade** CUP, Cambridge

Sassen S. (1991) **The Global City: New York, London, Tokyo** Princeton University Press, Princeton, New Jersey

Short J. (1989) 'Yuppies, yuffies and the new urban order' **Transactions, Institute of British Geographers** NS 14, pp. 173–88

Simon B. (1992) 'Accountant opens books on a secret life' **The Financial Times** 5 June

Smith A. (1989) 'Gentrification and the spatial constitution of the state: the restructuring of London's Docklands' **Antipode** 21, pp. 232–60

Southwark Borough Planning Department (nd) **Broken Promises. The Southwark Experience of the LDDC** Southwark Council, London

Stephens P. (1991) 'Developer of Canary Wharf in plea to PM' **The Financial Times** 22 July

Thompson J. (1989) **Docklands Redevelopment. A Moral Dimension** Docklands Forum, London

Thrift N. J. (1989) 'The geography of international economic disorder', in R. J. Johnston and P. J. Taylor (eds.) **A World in Crisis? Geographical Perspectives** Blackwell, Oxford, 2nd edn, pp. 16–78

Tomkins R. (1991) 'Transport cash unloaded at Docklands' **The Financial Times** 6 September

US National Research Council, Committee on Waterfront Lands (1980) **Urban Waterfront Lands** National Academy of Sciences, Washington, DC

* Ward R (1986) 'London: the emerging Docklands city' **Built Environment** 12, pp. 114–27

* Weightman G. (1990) **London River** Guild Publishing, London

Widgery D. (1991) **Some Lives! A GP's East End** Sinclair-Stevenson, London

Willcock J. (1990) 'Property slump is worst since the war' **The Guardian** 20 November

* Williams S. (1990) **ADT Architecture Guide. Docklands** Architecture Design and Technology Press, London

* Zwingle E. (1991) 'Docklands. London's new frontier' **National Geographic** 180, 1, pp. 34–59